Spiritual

Abundance

JEREMY P. TARCHER • PUTNAM

a member of Penguin Putnam Inc.

NEW YORK

Spiritual Abundance

MEDITATIONS

AND AFFIRMATIONS

ON PROSPERITY

FOR EVERY DAY

OF THE YEAR

David Stuart Alexander

Most Tarcher/Putnam books are available at special quantity discounts for bulk purchases for sales promotions, premiums, fund-raising, and educational needs. Special books or book excerpts also can be created to fit specific needs. For details, write or telephone Putnam Special Markets, 200 Madison Avenue, New York, NY 10016; (212) 951-8891.

JEREMY P. TARCHER/PUTNAM
a member of Penguin Putnam Inc.
200 MADISON AVENUE
NEW YORK, NY 10016
http://www.putnam.com

Library of Congress Cataloging-in-Publication Data

Alexander, David Stuart.
Spiritual abundance / David Stuart Alexander.
p.   cm.
ISBN 0-87477-885-9 (alk. paper)
1. Self-realization—Religious aspects—Meditations.
2. Devotional calendars. 3. Affirmations. I. Title.
BL624.2.A42   1997   97-1286 CIP
158.1′28—dc21

BOOK DESIGN BY DEBORAH KERNER
COVER DESIGN BY RANDALL FREISEN
FRONT COVER IMAGE COURTESY OF DYNAMIC GRAPHICS

Printed in the United States of America
1   3   5   7   9   10   8   6   4   2
This book is printed on acid-free paper. ∞

To Joan, my soulmate, who lovingly demonstrated to me how the writing process can be a joyful, gentle flow.

Foreword

There are countless ways to walk a spiritual path—the path that leads us home to God. Many religions say, "Ours is the only way." But there is not just one way. There is the way that is right for you now, at this time and place where you are expressing your life.

Throughout the years I have heard countless people speak of wanting more fulfillment in their lives. They desire a greater degree of peace and long for a sense of acceptance, an all-embracing experience of love. The one common denominator I have found among seekers, from the most conservative to the broadly liberal, is the desire to have one's life experience be different and improved next month or next year from what it is today. In order for this to occur, an individual must be willing to do the work, to take the step in the direction of his or her desired good.

Spiritual Abundance offers a clear and simple yet wise and reflective way to journey through the year, traveling along an ever-expanding path toward greater and greater degrees of love, peace, and joy. Such fulfilling states do not just happen to a fortunate few. They are the natural result of a committed spiritual practice. This book will provide you with solid guidelines to help you step out on that path.

Since you are holding *Spiritual Abundance* in your hands right now, perhaps you are truly ready to take the next step on your path of attaining greater wisdom, growing from smallness and limitation into fulfillment and abundance. The time to achieve your goal is set by you. The power to live the kind of spiritually aware life you have dreamed of already lives within you. It need not be difficult unless you choose for it to be so. It can be a joyous adventure into what is possible.

Over twenty years ago I made a decision to study a spiritual lesson daily. I have remained true to this commitment with only a handful of "days off." My commitment to me has made a world of wondrous differences in my life. It can do the same for you. *Spiritual Abundance* offers you a gentle daily reminder that can make a world of wondrous differences in your life. But you have to make the commitment to your own spiritual growth.

To commit to a year of daily practicing of these simple ideas is to make a conscious commitment to your own spiritual awakening, a commitment to gently guiding your mind into the truth of its ultimate reality as a powerful, beloved son or daughter of God. The thought for each day will assist you in remembering who you are and who your Father/Mother God is.

Welcome this concise book as your constant companion for this year. Use it as laid out consecutively or at your own "random" selection. Mindfully apply the thought for the day to yourself and everyone you encounter or think of, and you will soon notice a shift in your perceptions of yourself and all others.

Who is David Stuart Alexander? He embodies a clear consciousness that understands the laws of spirit and living spiritually twenty-four hours a day. David brings forth true love for the individual in his writing and his living. He offers crystal clarity in his teaching and is a blessing to all the lives he touches. After ten years of marriage I still thank God daily that he is my soulmate and husband, and that together we are walking on the path home to God.

—Joan Gattuso

Introduction

We all seem to live our lives accompanied by an almost undefinable partner called "time." It appears to walk in lockstep with us from the day we are born. When we are younger and crave to be older, we want it to speed up. When we are older and yearn to be younger, we pray it will slow down. When we are engaged in our least favorite task of painting a room, time drags. When we are with the love of our lives having a wondrous evening, time flies.

We measure time. We are early; we are on time; we are late. Our entire feeling nature gets tied up in time. Our friendships, our jobs, our recreation all revolve around time. Time seems to be an unyielding tsar creating anxiousness, worry, stress, a feeling of lack. Few of us view time as friend.

If we have been on this planet for a while, we can see what we assume to be the effects of time on our bodies in the form of wrinkles, sagging skin, flabby muscles, graying, thinning hair. Our stamina isn't what it once was. As time passes, it seems to be the creator of more and more aches and pains.

Yet there are some spiritual folks among us who have a different view of time. They see it and all its supposed effects as an illusion over which we have control. They see that to be truly connected with one's Creator, God, one must begin to use time in a different way. They understand that the free will we all possess gives us power over time, rather than the other way around.

These folks are no different from you or me; they just see themselves differently in relationship to time. They see time as a spiritual tool.

They see time as abundance. And they use time accordingly. They are committed to using it each day to affirm their love, their power, their joy, their peace—their spiritual abundance.

And you can do the same. All it takes is a loving commitment to yourself and your inner divinity throughout the year. You will read each brief statement for every day, concluding with the affirmation. Then repeat each affirmation to yourself throughout the day at least twenty-five times. Whenever you have an extra moment in time to spare, close your eyes and experience the feeling the affirmation brings to you. And remember to stay in gratitude by saying, Thank you, God! for all the blessings that appear in your life.

Each month has a theme, and each day of each month is titled. You may choose to begin on January 1 and proceed through the year. But it may be perfect for you to take any month, or any day for that matter, and begin with it. Whatever your needs are, whatever you resonate with, will be the ideal place and time for you to begin. It is an easy process, however you decide to begin. But . . . you do have to be committed to yourself, to life, to change, to growth. If your life is less than you would have it be, this simple daily process can change it with ease.

When you begin to experience fully the abundance that a spiritual connection brings, you will also realize what a good "time" you've been having. Happy affirming.

JANUARY

*

Goals

January 1

New Beginnings

> We begin this new year filled with
> excitement and hope. We let the
> past go, never again to be limited by
> its teachings. We use the past only
> for its positive lessons as we gladly
> turn toward the future. We step for-
> ward with glad resolve in our goal
> setting.

Affirmation

> My goals fill me with joy and are
> achieved easily.

January 2

Certainty

The path to our personal abundance is certain when we connect with our creator. We embrace our goals for this season and infuse them with Divine power flowing through each of us. This strength fills us to happy overflowing this day and in all the days to come.

Affirmation

I turn to God my Creator for certain abundance.

January 3

Perfect Action

> What we do to achieve what we
> want is easy when we relax and let
> our actions always reflect our goals.
> We simply sit in a quiet spot, focus
> on what we wish to achieve, and
> know positively that our results will
> be for our highest good. We may do
> this as many times throughout the
> day as we feel the need.

Affirmation

> My actions always lead me to my
> goals.

January 4

Visualization

We easily reach what we want by seeing it in our mind's eye. If it is a thing or an object, we add three dimensions to it—color, size, shape, texture, brand name, location, etc. If it is an attitude, we see ourselves in a situation in a happy frame of mind exhibiting our new attitude.

Affirmation

I achieve what I want by seeing it.

January 5

Positive Thought

The ego part of us may spout negative litanies from time to time. Our responsibility is simply to replace each negativity with positivity. When we liberally sprinkle our goals with positive thought-forms, we achieve what we want rapidly. And the process becomes much more joyful.

Affirmation

My positive thoughts bring me what I want quickly.

January 6

Creative Connection

> We all need creativity, a new way of
> looking at life, to fully realize our
> wishes and desires. When we allow
> our beings to connect with God
> throughout the day, we rid ourselves
> of this awesome responsibility of
> doing everything ourselves and al-
> low the Universal creative process
> to flow through us.

Affirmation

> My creativity always comes from
> God.

January 7
Peacefulness

Our true accomplishments in life come when we are peaceful. Meditation, or sitting quietly, for at least fifteen minutes at the start of each day will assist us in reaching our creative (God) center. We then move into the day with ease and sureness, seeing challenges as minor inconveniences rather than gigantic blocks.

Affirmation

God works his wonders through me when I am peaceful.

January 8

Attraction

Our countenance is like a magnet as we move through life. Whatever we feel, whatever we project is what we attract to us. That's why, in the process of reaching our goals, we need to extend to others what we want to receive ourselves every minute of every day. We then must extend love to all.

Affirmation

I attract love because love is who I am.

9

January 9

Anticipation

If we will but await the results of
what we want in excited anticipation, we will speed the process of
achievement along. Anticipation
adds Divine juice to our goals, giving us the energy to provide whatever action is needed day to day. It
also helps keep us connected at all
times to our Source.

Affirmation

I anticipate my highest good every
moment.

January 10
Freedom

Freedom is a state of mind. If we don't feel free to do what is necessary, we lose our enthusiasm. On the other hand, when we feel unlimited freedom, our creative process flows with ease. Our freedom is guaranteed us by God, and it is simply up to us to use its limitlessness as we move toward our goals.

Affirmation

I am free; therefore I am unlimited.

January 11

Joy

When we feel joy in our lives, there is literally nothing we cannot accomplish. All we need to remember is that joy does not come from others or outer circumstances. It comes from our Creator. Living in a state of joy allows us to appreciate every person, every thing, every moment.

Affirmation

My joy brings me exactly what I want.

January 12

Harmony

Our goals are achieved with ease when we are in harmony with all of existence. We must be in harmony with nature, in our personal relationships, with ourselves, and with God. The harmony that we feel is not bestowed upon us. It is our birthright. And it is up to us to live in a harmonious state.

Affirmation

I am in harmony with every aspect of my life.

January 13

Free Will

> God gave us free will. That means
> we can do or be or say anything we
> can imagine whenever we choose.
> We can allow free will to work for us
> or against us as we move toward
> our goals. What we have to remem-
> ber at all times is that no one else
> makes us do anything. It is always
> *our* choice.

Affirmation

> I use my free will to make perfect
> choices.

January 14

Movement

Movement is synonymous with change in our lives. As we travel toward what we want, we must change. Our movement may take the form of new ideas or a new residence or new friends. Whatever its form, we need to embrace movement in order to get to our goals.

Affirmation

I embrace movement to achieve my goals.

January 15

Openness

When we are open to whatever occurs in our lives, we can learn from
every experience. If we close down
to what shows up, we cannot. An
open attitude allows us to see every
event as a learning opportunity.
This same attitude will keep us going precisely where we want to go
every moment.

Affirmation

I am fully open to every experience.

January 16

Remembering

We all come from God. When we remember our Divine Source, we are able to release much of the onus of life that we feel. Our Source always directs us if we will but let Her do so. Remembering this gives us the freedom to accomplish whatever we wish with a great deal of ease.

Affirmation

Today I remember that I come from God.

January 17

Divine Assistance

Our Creator is always there to assist us. The voice for God will guide us in every situation if we are open to it. We can pray, meditate, simply have a conversation with God. We need to remember that we are one with God. We are not separate from Him. We can always allow God to speak through us.

Affirmation

God always gives me assistance.

January 18

Re-creation

Sometimes when we have worked with our goals for a while, they no longer seem to fit or even be what we desire. It is perfect to give ourselves permission to alter or even completely change our goals. All this means is that we are growing beyond the need to have these goals and now deserve new ones.

Affirmation

I change my goals easily.

January 19

Clarity

During the process of achieving our goal, we may find that our reason for selecting it in the first place has become fuzzy. What this means is that we probably have gotten so involved in the process that we have forgotten where our goal is supposed to take us. When that occurs, we just ask for God's guidance to clarify our goal for us.

Affirmation

My goal is always completely clear to me.

January 20

Divine Order

> There is Divine Order in every-
> thing we do. If we lose track of what
> that is, we need to sort out just
> what needs to be done next and
> next and next. We do this with
> God's assistance at every step. If
> we struggle, we are coming from
> ego. If we flow, we are coming from
> Divine Inspiration.

Affirmation

> God keeps my life in Divine Order.

January 21

Focus

If our goal seems to be taking an inordinate amount of time, perhaps we have been sidetracked by other, insignificant wants and desires. Every day, as frequently as possible, we must maintain our focus on what we wish to achieve. When we do, we move swiftly toward our desired end.

Affirmation

I remain focused and achieve my goal quickly.

January 22

Timing

We keep trying and trying and nothing happens. That means we have put ourselves in charge instead of God. Indeed, timing for all events in our lives comes from Divine Inspiration, not ego force. If we simply keep God and our goals in mind, our goals will come to pass when it is perfect that they do so.

Affirmation

My goals manifest at the perfect time.

January 23

Fine-tuning

Our fondest desire looks almost the way we want it to—but not quite. An earlier we would have accepted this as okay. But now we know we deserve the best, that if we are satisfied with a goal partially manifested we are demeaning ourselves. We stay with our desire until it is exactly as we want it to be.

Affirmation

I deserve and accept only the best.

January 24

Seeing

Our visualization techniques have taken us to the point where we see our goal with a clarity never before imagined. This is the step just before we accomplish precisely what we want. Seeing to this degree moves us easily to our final creation. It is now just a baby step to completion.

Affirmation

I clearly see my realized goal.

January 25

Sharing

During the process of reaching goals, there are times when you wish to share your progress with others. We need to do this discriminately, only with those friends, relatives, and teachers in our lives who we are 100 percent certain will support us fully. And remember, God always fully supports us.

Affirmation

I share my goals only with those who always support me.

January 26

Unity

> We know we are in sight of completing our goal when we unite with it. That is, what our goal represents and who we are are indistinguishable. We have been so focused that our nearly finished achievement is fully integrated into our lives. A feeling of elation (not obsession) is what always accompanies us at this stage.

Affirmation

> My goal and my purpose in life are identical.

January 27
Rejoicing

It is very helpful at any time for us to rejoice in our progress toward accomplishing what we want in life. It is particularly helpful to do so when we are near the end of our quest. Allowing joy to encircle us and our goal helps us know that what we want is Divinely inspired and will greatly aid us and all of humankind.

Affirmation

I rejoice in my life and in my goals.

January 28

Completion

> There is nothing so gratifying in life as the completion of goals we have worked with for weeks, months, or even years. We need to make certain we take those last steps with certainty so that our goals become a fact in our lives. As soon as one is accomplished, another Divinely backed goal will soon arise for us to accomplish.

Affirmation

> I complete my goal with ease.

January 29

Releasing

Once we have completed a goal, we need to release any and all attachment to it. It may have served us well, but further connection with it puts us in the past and stands in the way of our hearing the Voice for God and moving toward another achievement in our lives.

Affirmation

I joyfully release my completed goal.

January 30

God Connection

We need to remember at all times where our goal came from, particularly when we are between goals. Whatever our inspiration has been and will be comes from God. In order to step forward into the next exciting phase of our lives we must connect with our Creator as often as possible. We can make this connection any time of the day.

Affirmation

Throughout the day I remember that God is my source.

January 31

Thanks

Living in a state of thankfulness keeps us aware of and connected to our Source. When we feel gratitude, we feel the joy in all of life. When we feel gratitude, we feel the peace in all of life. When we feel gratitude, we feel the love in all of life. Gratitude gives us the power to live life fully.

Affirmation

Thank you, God! Thank you, God! Thank you, God!

FEBRUARY

Love

February 1

Discovery

Love does not reside in some mysterious realm outside us. It lives within us all the time. For love to lead an active life within us, however, we must discover its presence. We do this by releasing our blocks to love through forgiving ourselves and others for every misstep we perceive we or they have taken.

Affirmation

I discover love's presence through forgiveness.

February 2

Self

How we practice love and what we know about love must start with ourselves. We need to connect with our inner Divinity and allow that power to guide us to the true meaning of love. We will be able to love others in our lives to the extent that we can love ourselves.

Affirmation

I allow the God in me to show me love.

Family

Virtually all of us learned how to be loving and unloving through our family upbringing. It is extremely important for us to focus on all the wonderful lessons we gained from our mothers, fathers, siblings, and all our other relatives. We are still learning, and we must remember to return love for those valuable lessons.

Affirmation

I give love to every family member.

February 4

Friends

As we reach adulthood, we usually have an ever-increasing circle of friends. Our friends may be more unpredictable than the family we are used to. These differences offer us the opportunity to practice loving in broader strokes than ever before. Our friends are as deserving of love as we and anyone else are.

Affirmation

My friends offer me greater opportunities to love.

February 5

Animals

The creatures of our wondrous planet deserve love as much as we do. We can practice loving our dog, our cat, our canary, our goldfish just as we can practice loving ourselves and others. We can also extend love to the wild creatures of Mother Earth, since their struggle to survive is much more intense than ours.

Affirmation

My love flows to all animals.

February 6

Plants

It may seem odd, but plants can receive love just as people and animals can. And directing love toward the flowers, the trees, the bushes during the course of the day helps keep us in a loving posture all the day through. When we practice on our houseplants, we can see the results in the form of healthy, increased growth.

Affirmation

I send love to all plant life.

February 7
Creation

There is no greater creation in life than loving. Love always exists, but the creative part is to allow it to flow through us every moment, even at times when we don't feel a situation calls for a loving response. When we allow Universal Love to be expressed through us, we create magic in our lives.

Affirmation

I allow myself to express love every moment.

February 8

Sharing

After we have gotten ourselves in a space of love, there is no greater joy than sharing it. We can share it with our family, our friends, our pets, our plants. Since there is no limit to love, we can watch it grow as we share it. We can also watch others return the favor to us as we move through the day.

Affirmation

My life works when I share love.

February 9

Possibilities

There is perhaps no greater joy in life than exploring all the possibilities presented to us by love. We feel our God connection more fully. We see the love of a baker in a piece of toast. We lovingly wrap ourselves in warm clothes. We lovingly marvel at our bodies and how they work as we walk down the street. We love the stars.

Affirmation

There is no limit to the possibilities of love in my life.

February 10
Purpose

We seem to pursue many purposes
in life, but all are meaningless unless we approach any purpose with
a loving attitude. When we are on
the right track with our purpose, we
approach it always with loving joy.
If our purpose seems to be a struggle, then we need to examine it carefully, probably changing it.

Affirmation

My life's purpose is filled with love.

February 11
Every Day

To complete each day of our life
with richness, we fill every day with
love. From the time we arise in the
morning, we turn our first thoughts
to love. Then as we move through
the day, we approach every decision, every challenge with a loving
thought. Then our lives work effortlessly.

Affirmation

I fill every day with love.

44

February 12

Wonder

Sunsets, new life, sweet smells, soft touches all can fill us with wonder. The more we allow ourselves to be in touch with wonder, the more we are in touch with the loving side of us. The Divine love that resides equally in each of us sparks deep feelings of awe for ourselves, for others, for life itself.

Affirmation

I live my life in loving wonder.

45

February 13

Joy

This day when we begin our job—whether at home or in an office or elsewhere—which fills a great portion of our day, we allow the joy of what we do bubble to the surface. When we feel the joy of accomplishment, we are in touch with the law of right action in our lives. Joy brings us love. Love brings us joy.

Affirmation

My joy of doing puts me in touch with love.

February 14

Romance

Romantic love with another truly is what makes the world go 'round. Strife of every description melts away when we are with our lover. When we give love, when we receive love, our cares seem insignificant indeed. Our being overflows with life at those times of deep, abiding love with another.

Affirmation

Today I share total love with my partner.

February 15

Inclusive

Our lives are infused with all kinds of love, and then our lives work perfectly. We include love in everything we think, say, or do, and we breeze through each day smiling at everyone and everything. All we need to do is to remember that it is our choice alone that brings love its all-inclusiveness.

Affirmation

I include love in everything I think, say, or do.

February 16
Enveloping

Love wraps us in its soft caresses
when we allow it to do so. We can
be in any situation and see it as one
that challenges us with fear or envelops us with love. *Love* is an active verb that creates whirlwinds of
soft feeling whose vortexes are always there for us to step into. We
are always the one who decides for
love.

Affirmation

Today I allow love to envelop me.

February 17

Extending

We sometimes feel erroneously that for us to have love it must be bestowed upon us. That is not the case. Love is always with us in limitless quantities, and for us to feel it more and more we must extend love to others. By extending love we can change any situation. By extending love we are declaring ourselves to be loving people.

Affirmation

I extend love to everyone in every situation.

February 18

Lessons

Love is a gentle, persistent teacher from whom we can learn many wondrous lessons. We can turn around any unpleasant situation that may arise by seeking its lesson of love. When we move through each day feeling the love in ourselves, we are then an open student to the teacher called "Love."

Affirmation

I am open to every lesson of love.

February 19

Hugs

Hugging someone can be a marvelous physical sharing of love. We must first come from a space of love and be certain the other person is receptive before giving a hug. When we hug someone and are coming from a deep, loving space, we always feel the love being returned to us. The feeling is something akin to heaven.

Affirmation

My hugs are given with pure love.

February 20

Release

Love is the great releaser of negativity. It is impossible for us to be in an unhappy state of mind when we feel love. Love must and does stand alone and doesn't allow for anything unlike itself to enter. To release the burdens felt from any situation, we turn to the Divine love within and allow them to fly away.

Affirmation

I release my problems through love.

February 21

Healing

There is no greater physician we can turn to than God and Her Love. The healing power of love is phenomenal in the realms of both mental and physical challenges. When we are in a position that calls for healing, we must call upon love. If we slip into negativity, we must gently and continuously bring ourselves back to God's Love.

Affirmation

The Love of God heals me.

February 22

Unifying

With the world seemingly in a state of disrepair, the unifying aspect of love is the only way to bring it back to wholeness. We do this by focusing on our own lives and remembering that love unites us with our family, friends, acquaintances, and even those people we have never met and probably never will.

Affirmation

Love unifies me with everyone.

February 23
Truth

Many of us spend a great deal of our lives seeking truth. There is only one truth: love. When we seek love, we find it and we find truth as well. For love injected into any area of life reveals its truth. The search for truth is not in vain, however, for if we persist we will always discover love.

Affirmation

Love brings me to truth.

February 24

Faith

> Faith in the God within us all is how
> we keep in touch with love. There is
> no empirical proof for faith. It is part
> of our state of beingness. Whether
> we follow the tenets of a specific
> religion or we simply "know" God,
> our constant faith awakens the
> awareness of love in us.

Affirmation

> My faith awakens my love.

February 25

Light

Our love is often represented by light. Some of us see visions of light, a holy light that permeates our essence. This light is comforting, appeasing, nurturing, and contains all the fullness of love. Light leads to love, and love leads to light. When we see the light in others, we know love's light is blossoming in ourselves.

Affirmation

When I see light, I see love.

February 26

Strength

All the strength in all the people in all the universe comes from love. It is not helpful if we confuse strength with physical prowess. Strength is certainty, a knowing that emanates from our loving core. When we live our lives exhibiting strength in its true form, we are really demonstrating the power of love.

Affirmation

Love is my true strength.

February 27
Unconditional

Authentic love is unconditional. Whenever we place conditions on any situation, we remove the love from it. Unconditional love means giving love to a person or an event regardless of appearances. Unconditional love is the love that flows from God throughout the universe of life. It is always ours.

Affirmation

I feel the unconditional Love of God.

February 28

God

God's Love is all there is. We humans have done all we can to change ourselves and the shape of our planet, but we've usually made these alterations with motives that were unlike love. When we work with the unlimited supply of God's Love that is always ours to use, everybody in every circumstance wins.

Affirmation

I am one with the limitless Love of God.

MARCH

❦

Happiness

March 1

Choice

Our happiness is always a choice,
though it does not always seem so.
When we step into our center, we
see happiness occurring through us,
not being thrust upon us. We select happiness moment to moment.
When we feel fear or sadness, we
simply need to choose once again.
And we can choose happiness.

Affirmation

Today I choose happiness every
moment.

March 2

Observation

> When we observe happiness in others, we are able to embrace it more easily ourselves. We can always see the joy in everything if we want to. It is a simple task for us to watch the world and connect with its happiness, for that feeling is always alive and well within us.

Affirmation

> I see happiness everywhere and in everything.

March 3

Relaxation

Happiness is not a feeling we can easily make contact with when we are tense or out of sorts. We need to relax into it. Our joy fills us easily when we are relaxed. Taking a moment at any time during the day to be at ease will allow our happiness to bubble up within us. Our relaxation is our door to happiness.

Affirmation

I relax and I am happy.

March 4
Home

Being at home either in the physical sense or in our hearts can make us happy. Our brick-and-mortar homes remind us of the joys of the security of childhood. But we can literally be anywhere on our planet and feel the pleasure of "home" in our hearts. Our God within is always our home.

Affirmation

I am home; therefore I am happy.

March 5
Workplace

Most of us have jobs we attend to in our lives. For us to be whole and complete, we need to find joy in our work and workplace. So we must first do what makes us happy, and then make that our lifework. We simply listen to our inner guidance and then follow it to our happiness in our work.

Affirmation

My work always gives me joy.

March 6

Interacting

A great portion of each day is spent in interacting with our environment and with others. We can always make these interactions pleasant ones. Even if we are upset with another person or a situation, we can transform these emotions by infusing them with joyous feelings we bring up from our inner selves.

Affirmation

I interact with my world happily.

March 7

Imagination

If we will but allow it to be so, our imagination is an easy guide to happiness. We don't live in a fantasy world, but we allow our minds to wander joyously in the present as we plan for a delightful future. We need only be in a peaceful state of mind with little or no distraction to let our imagination go.

Affirmation

I allow my imagination to lead me to happiness.

March 8

Awe

Our universe becomes an incredibly delightful place when we allow ourselves to feel awestruck by it. Living our lives in awe means moving through each day with smiles on our faces. We can experience the wonder in literally everything we see and do if we simply let the past go and remain in the now.

Affirmation

Every moment fills me with awe.

March 9
Enchantment

When we watch children play, we can see their happiness arising from the enchantment they feel at practically all their real and imagined experiences. We can do the same if we return to the child within us, seeing the angels in the clouds, smelling the perfume of all plants, feeling the God in us.

Affirmation

I am enchanted by the joy of life.

March 10
Dreams

Many of us are visited by dreams every evening, while some of us dream actively during the day. These dreams all can become messages of happiness. We need only to relax into them and see that they are giving us tools for joyful living, even if some seem frightening at the time. We must always embrace our dreams.

Affirmation

My dreams are keys to happiness.

March 11

Planning

Our plans lead us to the future, and our thoughts are our plans. It is important that our thoughts always be happy, God-connected ones, because we will create a future like our present. Whether we are actively planning or whether we believe we are simply letting our minds wander, we need to ensure that our thoughts are happy.

Affirmation

I plan with God and a joyful mind.

March 12
Manifesting

We know that thoughts are things, so when we are thinking we are manifesting in the outer world. All we need to do is look at what is arising in our lives to know whether or not we are manifesting from a happy place. We simply need to take responsibility for all that shows up so we can alter anything that is less than delightful.

Affirmation

I manifest only happy results.

March 13

Appreciation

Life flows for us so much more easily when we live from a state of appreciation. And it is easy to live this way. All we need to do is be aware of everything in our outer and inner realms every moment. We must really look at life, smell life, touch life, embrace life. Then we will have a happy appreciation of all that is.

Affirmation

I fully appreciate all of life.

March 14

Quiet

God is in the stillness. All of our creation comes from that quiet place within us. To reach that place we need to find a secluded spot, close our eyes, and allow our thoughts to drift away. We release all attachment to our thoughts for ten minutes or longer if possible. We can then connect with the God within.

Affirmation

I find God in the quiet within me.

March 15

Humanity

We deal with other people virtually every day of our lives, and we react to them with either fear or love. Whichever arises within us is our choice. What makes life totally fulfilling is our seeing happiness in everyone. They may not be manifesting it at the moment, but we can look beneath their veneer and feel their innate joy.

Affirmation

I experience the joy in all of humanity.

March 16

Family

How many of us have blamed many of our woes on our families—our parents, our siblings, our aunts and uncles? At this stage of our lives, it is time for us to change this attitude to a positive one. They all did the best they could, and now it is time for us to find the blessings and see all our family experiences as growing ones.

Affirmation

My family brings me nothing but happiness.

March 17

Self

When we awaken in the morning and stand in front of the mirror in the bathroom, we must see beyond that bleary-eyed countenance to the joyful being. We need to treat ourselves as kindly as we want others to treat us. Within ourselves is contained all the happiness of the Universe, and it is our choice to block it or to allow it to fully express.

Affirmation

I express the joy that I am.

March 18
Earth

We very often take Mother Earth for granted, but if we pause a moment to reflect we realize that her support is what makes our life experience so complete. We cannot help but be joyous when we realize the amazing balance of air, water, gravity, and all her elements that sustain our lives. We thank God for her support.

Affirmation

I delight in the blessings of Mother Earth.

March 19

Success

Our success in life comes from our joyous inner core. It arises from our awareness of the God within. When we observe individuals who have apparent outer success but are not happy, we know that they have no success at all. The success that we have in this life experience *is* happiness. All the rest is frosting on the cake. It really doesn't matter.

Affirmation

My happiness is my success.

March 20
Activity

The activity in all our lives some-times seems to be meaningless. It is when we are active with joy that meaning arises. Before we begin any activity, we need to do a frame-of-mind check. Are we happy? If not, we need to take time to release all negative thoughts before com-mencing any action.

Affirmation

I am happy in all my activities.

March 21
Touch

Physical touch reminds us that we are human. We may shy away from touch if we come from a mentally or physically abusive background, but we can experience real joy through a simple hug or even a touch on the shoulder. We may think of touch as a happy God experience that connects us with others on the physical level.

Affirmation

Touching and being touched always gives me pleasure.

March 22

Sound

If we listen to the sounds of life, we help round ourselves into happy beings. Even if we are deaf, we can always hear the sound of the Voice for God directing our every action. As we glide through the day, we simply listen to every sound, knowing that each sound leads us to joy.

Affirmation

The sounds of life give me joy.

March 23

Sight

When we look at all life has to offer,
we are happy indeed. Even with
physical blindness our God sight is
still in place. We can choose to see
everything with pleasure instead of
pain. Our faculty of sight is a mar-
velous asset to our total human experience. We need to use it in joy.

Affirmation

My happiness is reflected through
my sight.

March 24

Beauty

The real beauty of life is our ability to see beauty in all of life. When we do, we bring happiness to ourselves and others. If we see other than the loveliness of a person or a situation, we must simply know there is beauty existing there. We must always take the time to appreciate all beauty to complete our own happiness.

Affirmation

I see beauty in all of life.

March 25

Flow

> Life truly flows like a river. We can either flow with the current or battle it by trying to swim upstream. The flow is Divine Order, and we don't have to do anything to experience it. We must merely accept it. Our acceptance of the flow of life is the key to our happiness.

Affirmation

> The flow of life gives me joy.

March 26

Contentment

For us to be content it is important that we accept ourselves as we are and accept the world as it is. This doesn't mean we don't grow and help to better our planet. It simply means we live fully in every moment and drink in its fullness. When we do, we become happily content with everything.

Affirmation

I am content with myself and my world.

March 27

Support

We come from our God space when we give mental and emotional support to ourselves and others. Our world is a mutually supportive place. All we have to do is to tune in to our inner guidance and lend support whenever and wherever needed. Giving unconditional support gives us joy.

Affirmation

I happily support myself and others.

March 28

Caring

Caring is an aspect of ourselves that broadens us. When we care about what happens to others, to our city, to our country, to our world, we fill ourselves with happy thoughts and experiences. Caring comes from our Divinity, our deep loving place, our concern for the completeness of life. Caring equals love equals happiness.

Affirmation

I am caring; therefore I am happy.

March 29
Positive

When we have positive thoughts, we have happy thoughts. When we are positive, we easily attract everything we desire in life. When we are positive, we affect everyone we know in a joyous manner. When we are positive, we create a beautiful world. When we are positive, we are connected to God.

Affirmation

My happiness comes from my positive attitudes.

March 30

Prayer

Our prayers do make a difference
for all the life on our world. We
don't beseech God, we affirm with
Him what we know to be the
truth. We are co-creators with God,
and our prayers simply affirm Her
power and connection with us. It is
our praying that finally leads us to
complete happiness.

Affirmation

I connect with God through prayer.

March 31
God-Centered

Whether we realize it or not, we are God-centered beings. We are Divine creatures, even though our humanity may seem to belie that at times. When we live from our God center, we feel complete. The only true happiness that awaits us comes from our God center. The God center of us is who we are.

Affirmation

My total happiness comes from my God center.

APRIL

Growth

April 1

Spiritual

We can grow spiritually each day of our lives. All we need to do is focus on our Creator more and more often. What we discover is that the thing we perceive as spiritual growth is really our personalities getting out of the way of our true natures. We then let God come through us and allow our spirituality to soar.

Affirmation

I grow spiritually every day.

April 2

Mental

Our mental capacities help us function effectively in our day-to-day routines. It is important to nurture our mental capabilities to keep us fully in balance. But we also must ever realize that improving only the "head" side of us will not serve to make us whole people. We need to keep our mental growth in perspective.

Affirmation

I thank God for mental growth.

April 3
Feeling

We know we are alive when we let our feeling side free. We are not all feeling, but the portion of us that is helps balance our mental nature and allows us to express our spirituality effectively. Our feelings connect us with others. It is through our feeling nature that we express love.

Affirmation

I am aware of my true feelings today.

April 4

Observation

Our powers of observation on all levels keep us aware of our connection with all of life. We can use our seeing as a tool to better our existence. If we don't like the way we see our lives, we can change them. If we do like what we observe, we can do more of the same. Observation is awareness.

Affirmation

My growing powers of observation connect me with all of life.

April 5

Commitment

What is commitment? It is saying we are going to do something, then doing it, saying we are going to be something, then being it. Commitment is a method to move us to fullness of purpose in life. When we fail to keep our commitments, our life stumbles. When we keep our commitments, our life wondrously expands.

Affirmation

I increase my commitment to myself and others.

April 6
Right Action

Sometimes we have to choose the best direction, which will serve all concerned in any situation. When we pursue right action, we select personal growth for ourselves and caring for others. Right action may not always be clear, but it is important that we strive for it in every event of our lives.

Affirmation

Today I choose right action.

April 7
Play

All work and no play . . . We know the rest. For us to make progress in our lives, we must take time to do those things for ourselves that have no evident purpose but give us pleasure. Play helps lighten us and assists us in putting all of life in perspective. When we take time for play, we take time to love ourselves.

Affirmation

I enjoy playing in the world.

April 8

Ease

> Struggle tells us that we are coming
> from our ego and not our God-self.
> The God in us makes life easy for
> us. When we are connected to our
> Source, our decisions come with
> ease, and our follow-up action lead-
> ing to positive results is effortless.
> It is helpful several times a day to
> ensure we are proceeding through
> life with ease.

Affirmation

> I accomplish everything I want with
> ease.

April 9

Health

We age, but our mental, emotional, and physical health doesn't have to. In fact, if we are living life in a growth mode, our health is getting better every day. If we have pain of any kind, it is important to immediately see ourselves as whole and complete just the way we are. If we are in a recovery mode, we must see ourselves as totally healed.

Affirmation

I live in perfect health.

April 10

Art

There's an artist living in every one of us. When we let that artist out—whether it's through music, photography, flower arranging, painting, decorating, or whatever—we nurture our soul's growth. It is important that we set aside time to pursue our artistic interests. When we do, we positively affect every area of our lives.

Affirmation

Today the artist in me flourishes.

April 11

Purpose

Pursuing our Divine purpose is how we continue to grow. Here's how you recognize your purpose: Do you love life? Do you love doing what you do? Are you doing what you do with love? If you answered "yes" to these questions, you are living your purpose. If "no," ask God daily for guidance until you have your answers.

Affirmation

I live totally in alignment with my purpose.

April 12

Sharing

Our success in this lifetime is rounded out when we share all we are, know, and have. When we share ourselves, we receive love and appreciation and continue on our path of growth. Since the world is a completely abundant place, sharing everything we have only increases what we have to share.

Affirmation

I happily share all my resources this day.

April 13

Parenting

When we have children, it is a delight to be a parent and lend them our expertise in life. Even if we do not have children, there are many times in each day when we are asked to give advice in a parental role. When we do so, let us remember to do so in love and by asking our God within for guidance.

Affirmation

God helps me be the perfect parent.

April 14

Respect

We must have respect for ourselves and others. We need to respect all of life. When we live from a place of respect, we allow ourselves to appreciate all the subtleties life affords us. We cannot come from a place of respect without coming from a place of love. Respect for everything allows us to expand in every aspect of life.

Affirmation

I wholly respect all of life.

April 15
Goodness

If we have ever criticized other people or institutions, we should remember that everyone and everything have goodness in them. What appears as evil is simply the blocks to love that our fears have created. It is our responsibility to see beyond the fears deep within to the goodness we all possess as a birthright.

Affirmation

Today I see the goodness in everything and everyone.

April 16

Laughter

We've just dented our pristine car's fender, and instead of lamenting we laugh at the situation. When we laugh at such times, we are telling the Universe we don't take our little travails seriously. We have life in proper growth perspective. Laughter frees us to learn with ease life's lessons. Since it's a choice, we might as well choose laughter.

Affirmation

I choose to laugh at all my problems.

April 17

Love

Whatever challenges we face in the course of a day, love brings us back to reality. We can look in the mirror and affirm love for ourselves. If we hear a harsh word from another, we can give love in return. We love our parents, our children, our friends. Love connects us to the very essence of life itself. Growth *is* love; love *is* growth.

Affirmation

Love brings me everything I want.

April 18
Teaching

As we move through life, we are often in a teaching mode. We can accept this role as one that flows from the God within and helps to expand us and those we are teaching at any moment. The marvelous aspect of being a teacher is that we learn at the same time. We then can embrace our teaching roles as Divinely inspired.

Affirmation

I lovingly teach through the God in me.

April 19

Following

When we let go of control and follow, life flows and we grow as a
result. It is important to let our
guidance lead the way, whether that
Divine direction shows up from
within us or from others who appear
in our lives. Being a follower gets us
in contact with our humbleness.

Affirmation

Today I let Divine guidance lead
the way.

April 20
Softness

Life often seems to demand that we have a hard edge. But it is our softness, our feminine side, that truly brings us to creation. Relaxing into what we want helps speed along all manifestation. We think of ourselves as a bed of feathers through which creativity flows with ease. Our softness guarantees that we will grow.

Affirmation

I show my softness to the world.

115

April 21
Excellence

It is crucial to us that we never settle for less than excellence in all things in our life. Allowing the mediocre in affirms that we are not deserving of the best. Seeking excellence in everything announces to God that we are Her perfect children. Our insisting on excellence for ourselves allows us to share the same with the world.

Affirmation

My life is filled with only excellence.

April 22

Focus

There is a place for daydreams, and there is a place for focus. If we wish to grow, to accomplish our desires, we must bring our entire beings into focus. We release all extraneous thoughts moment by moment to retain focus. We zero in on what we want and in short order manifest it. Our power expresses through our focus.

Affirmation

I focus 100 percent on what I want today.

April 23

Giving

Our Universe is limitless. It is fully abundant. Contrary to some beliefs, there are no shortages of anything. We can prove this by giving. We tithe to our church. We give freely of our love. We never cling to any object or idea. We give, give, give. What we then discover is that we still have abundance from which we can continue to give.

Affirmation

I give from my unlimited abundance.

April 24

Receiving

What is our worth by our own estimate? When we are given something, do we accept the gift with a smile or do we resist it? If we resist we are questioning our self-worth. On the other hand, if we receive happily, gratefully, we are telling the universe that we are deserving. Good receivers are always filled with love and growing.

Affirmation

Today I receive with joy and thanks.

April 25

Peace

> Peace is the result of our knowing
> that we are complete just the way
> we are, that the world is complete
> just the way it is. Being at peace
> doesn't mean we don't change; it
> means that we fully accept the way
> things are. In fact, when we are at
> peace change comes more easily.
> Peace is akin to love and comes from
> God.

Affirmation

> I am completely at peace this day.

April 26

Discovery

The joy of discovery makes life worth living. We grow when we are open to newness. We drive to work a different way and discover a whole new world. We read a book on a subject we've never studied before and open ourselves to new possibilities. We say hello to a stranger and make a new friend. Discovery makes our life crackle with excitement.

Affirmation

I discover the newness in my life.

April 27

Ascent

Life is an upward spiral, and we are on a glorious ascent to an enlightened state. There is nothing we have to do other than to allow it to be. We can block this rise, but it is so easy simply to let it happen. In a quiet state of mind we can visualize ourselves soaring on our life path and fully embracing our good, our God.

Affirmation

I soar on my ascent to God.

April 28
Unity

We truly grow when we experience the unity in everything. We open our consciousness to it all. Our sun, our planet, our neighbor, the oak tree in the forest, our cat, the green beans for dinner, the raging thunderstorm, ourselves—all are one. We can relish life by embracing this unity that is so all-encompassing.

Affirmation

I happily experience the unity in everything.

April 29

Purity

We look at a baby in a bassinet and see the purity of his soul. We arrive with that purity in us. It never diminishes, and our growth is simply reestablishing contact with it. One way to do this is to look for the purity in others. When we discover it, we can be certain it remains an essential part of our being.

Affirmation

My purity of soul expresses itself today.

April 30
Surrender

> Our world may appear to be threatening, but if we surrender to it we discover that God's Love is behind it all. When we surrender, we proclaim that God is in charge, not us. We surrender to the universal perfection that is God's Will. Surrender uncomplicates life for us by letting us live in the gentle, loving flow.

Affirmation

> Today I surrender to God's Will.

May

Kindness

May 1
Freedom

A feeling of kindness within us gives us the ultimate freedom to be and do what we want. We are able to leave guilt behind and become the full expression of who we truly are. Our freedom to think kind thoughts leads to kind acts. Kind acts in turn demonstrate to us that we are free. It is a joyous circle.

Affirmation

I am free because I am kind.

May 2

Contentment

How wonderfully content we feel when we come from a space of kindness! Our lives are whole and complete. We walk through life with peace in our hearts and certainty in our eyes. Contentment through kindness is the natural order of things. We practice kindness in all situations, and we live from our serene center.

Affirmation

My kindness brings me contentment.

May 3

Wholeness

Many of us struggle for much of our lives feeling insecure and incomplete. All we have to do is turn from inside to outside ourselves using a little kindness as we do, and miraculously our lives do an about-face. Connecting with the world through kindness makes us realize that we are whole beings.

Affirmation

Today I am made whole by reaching out to others.

May 4
Will

Whenever we are lacking in kindness, we simply need to apply the power of will to ourselves. What we must remember is that when we allow our will to be one with God's Will, the process becomes one of allowing rather than making it happen. With God's Will flowing through us, there is nothing we cannot accomplish.

Affirmation

I am kind through the Will of God.

May 5

Honor

> We honor ourselves when we practice kindness. Assisting anyone with the simplest task elevates us to a place of honor in the universe. Kindness allows us to witness just how honorable all of humanity is. When we see this, we practice more kindness. Then we see more honor, practice more kindness . . . and joyfully the pattern continues.

Affirmation

> I honor myself through my kindness.

May 6
Cheerfulness

Someone gives aid to another, and we see large smiles displayed by the giver and the recipient. Kindness is synonymous with cheerfulness. In order to be kind we must come from a space of joy. The cheer that we feel is the connection we all have with one another and with God. We merely express it through kindness.

Affirmation

I assist others cheerfully.

May 7
Gentleness

Although some of us don't always exhibit this trait, we are gentle creatures underneath it all. What better way to demonstrate this attribute than through kindness. Whether we are giving to ourselves or others, our gentle nature springs forth with kindness. Life is always easier when we live from our gentleness.

Affirmation

I nurture my gentle nature through kindness.

May 8
Celebration

Most of us can find any excuse to party. Why not celebrate the kind human beings that we are all becoming? There is no better reason for a celebration than the milk of human kindness. When we think about how we feel after performing a kind act, we realize it is celebrational in nature. Let us celebrate!

Affirmation

Today I celebrate my kindness.

May 9
Easy

Kindness is easy for us once we become used to living our lives without struggle. Life is much more difficult when we attempt to live it in isolation, rather than joining with and serving others. When we come from the God within, we easily unite with others, and performing acts of kindness is second nature to us.

Affirmation

It is easy for me to be kind.

May 10

Shelter

We think of our homes, our cars as shelter. But true shelter for us is the kind thoughts we have, the kind deeds we do. The divinity in us and others directs us to kindness, which in turn gives us shelter from our fears. As we feel sheltered by kindness, we can easily lend this feeling to others by being completely who we are.

Affirmation

Today my shelter is kindness.

May 11
Courage

Sometimes we believe courage is represented by heroic acts. But true courage is standing by the faith of our convictions through kindness. When we are kind we are courageous, for we can never step out timidly to be kind. It takes courage to get beyond any limits we place on ourselves to be of service to the world.

Affirmation

My kindness is made possible by my courage.

May 12

Betterment

Many people say this or that is for the betterment of the world. Kindness is almost never mentioned. But real betterment in our civilization will come only when a majority of us are concerned with kindness to our fellow humankind. To improve ourselves permanently we must be kind to ourselves and others.

Affirmation

I better my world through kindness.

May 13

Feeling

> We cannot think kindness; we must
> feel it. We cannot simply decide
> to be kind; we must embrace the
> thought with every fiber of our be-
> ing. Kind acts come from our feeling
> nature, which is our God nature.
> We feel kindness coming through us
> from God. We know we are feeling
> properly when we expect nothing in
> return.

Affirmation

> I thank God for my kind feelings.

May 14

Image

When we hold an image of ourselves, it is important that we hold a kind image. As the saying goes: Thoughts held in mind produce after their kind. An image of kindness that we visualize guides us gently to creating kind deeds as we move through life. If we stray from that image, we lovingly bring ourselves back to it.

Affirmation

I see myself as a kind person.

May 15

Excitement

Some people turn to artificial stimu-
lants for excitement, but there is
nothing more exciting for the soul
than a genuinely kind act. When we
are involved in kindnesses, we stim-
ulate ourselves in ways nothing artificial could ever do. We also create
a habit of kindness, which keeps us
continually on a path of excitement.

Affirmation

Today I am excited by my kind
deeds.

May 16

All-Encompassing

Kindness is all-encompassing. Kind people live longer, healthier, happier lives. Kind people are filled with love. Kind people are God-connected. Kind people are whole people. As we move from selfishness to selflessness, we begin to experience how all-encompassing this change can be.

Affirmation

I fill myself with kindness.

May 17
Luminous

We look at the face of a kind person, and we see a luminosity many of us have not yet experienced. Kindness is a God trait, and God is luminous. His light bathes us in kindness, and as we are kind we share the light with others. Luminous kindness then spreads from person to person throughout the world.

Affirmation

I am luminous because I am kind.

May 18

Influence

A lot of us think influence has to do with money and power. In reality the most influential people in the world are the kindest. Take Mother Teresa, for instance. Her unwavering kindness has directly or indirectly affected almost everyone on our planet. One single act of kindness gives us unlimited influence.

Affirmation

I am kind; therefore I am influential.

May 19

Direction

The self-centered person wanders our planet aimlessly. The kind person strides forth with sure direction. Kindness gives us purpose unlike any other trait. We will always discover a person, a situation in need of kindness. When we do and act on it, our life's direction becomes arrow-straight.

Affirmation

Today my kindness puts direction in my life.

May 20

Approval

When we remain within ourselves, we seek approval from others. When we live through kindness, our approval comes to us from God. Any generous, loving action carries with it its own approval, and we need no other. As kind individuals, we feel the approval of the wind and the earth, the birds and the fishes, all existence.

Affirmation

My kindness is its own approval.

May 21

Energy

> If we are lagging in our physical or mental energies, a kind act performed by us will change our feelings almost instantly. As we step outside ourselves to assist another, we will be energized. The energy that we feel is our unity with the universe. We are one with God and everyone, and kindness makes that energy-filled connection.

Affirmation

> I am energized through kindness.

May 22

Irresistible

There are many things in the world that are irresistible to us, not the least of which is kindness. But we have to practice it first to realize just how appealing it is. The attraction kindness holds comes from its Divine nature. We are coming from God when we act in kindness. And that feeling is impossible to resist.

Affirmation

Today I am drawn to kindness.

May 23

Pervasive

The wonderful thing about kindness is how all-pervasive it is. When we are kind, we feel completely wrapped in the arms of love. It enters our every thought. It permeates the very cells of our body. It envelops us with its totality. We become enraptured when we fill up with the effects of kindness.

Affirmation

I am completely filled with kindness.

May 24
Virtue

We are kind, thus we are virtuous. Virtue has many aspects, but kindness is among its most lovely. The virtue we have through kindness has nothing to do with ego and everything to do with God. Its Divine aspects direct us in every kind deed upon which we ever engage.

Affirmation

My virtue is kindness.

May 25

Essence

Kindness is akin to the essence of life, though it has its own essence as well. The essence of kindness is peace. The quiet of kindness may make it seem insignificant on the surface, but this essence comes from Universal Omnipotence, which makes it magnificent indeed. We need to remember daily the essence of kindness.

Affirmation

I live through the essence of kindness.

May 26
Vitality

If we weren't full and vital this morning when we arose, we may have forgotten kindness yesterday. Kindness fills us with vitality. It makes us replete with the fullness of life. A kind act, and another, remind us that we are one with everyone we help and that our strength comes from the boundless energy of God flowing through us.

Affirmation

Kindness fills me with vitality.

May 27

Awareness

Kindness leads us to awareness of the importance of what we do. This awareness arises from our inner divinity, our God connection. A kind act toward the "least" of us is as magnificent as any kindness, and we become fully aware that all benevolent acts are equally important.

Affirmation

My kind acts lead me to total awareness.

May 28

Completion

We can pursue spiritual paths endlessly, but until our pursuit is wrapped around kindness we won't achieve completion. Kindness is a facet of the diamond that we are that needs equal polishing with all the others. When we add kindness to our spiritual inventory, we take a giant step closer to spiritual completion.

Affirmation

My kind acts bring me closer to completion.

May 29
Self

We are not completely kind people unless we are kind to ourselves. In fact we cannot offer unconditional kindness to others unless we have kind, loving thoughts directed within. We need to do kind things for ourselves just as we do for others. This is not selfish. This is training to assist others.

Affirmation

Today I am kind to myself.

May 30
Others

Kindness to others makes us whole people. It announces to God that we know there is an abundance of love and kindness available to us all to share with all. That's why we pursue kind acts every day of the year. The kind deeds we do for others give us a feeling perhaps no other action can ever give us. They touch our totality.

Affirmation

I am kind to others in every situation.

May 31

God

God is kindness. Kindness is God. They are the same. A kind act is a God act. We are in touch with the Creator of all things every time we think a kind thought, share a kind word, do a kind deed. We pronounce our faith in God through kindness. Our kindnesses keep us connected with God each moment of each day.

Affirmation

My kindness connects me to God.

JUNE

Power

June 1

Intention

One of the most powerful tools we have at our disposal to manifest what we want in life is our intention. Its power is what makes things happen. Without intention we drift through life. The arrow of our intention lets our desire fly straight and true toward its target goal.

Affirmation

I place the power of intention behind what I want today.

June 2

Decision

Someone asks us what we want to eat, and our answer is: "I don't care." If we are then served worms, we realize we do care! We fully exercise our power when we make decisions, from the smallest to the largest. We have the gift of free will from God. That means we can decide exactly how we want life to present itself.

Affirmation

Today I make decisions easily.

June 3

Integrating

If we look at our life as containing many compartments, we are seeing it amiss. Our life is one life, and it is up to us to integrate all its parts into one powerful whole. We exist as individuals, but if we see ourselves as having a career part, a play part, a love part, a home part, a food part, etc., we can play one of these parts unhappily.

Affirmation

I live as a whole, happy being.

June 4

Beginning

Whether it's this day, a new project, a relationship, an idea, beginning is empowering. If we sidestep into newness, we dissipate our power. The power we have comes from God, and She fully backs us when we start anew. We let go of our past and live fully in the here and now when we use our power to begin.

Affirmation

I begin everything in my life fully empowered.

June 5

Action

The power of action stirs us up, makes us alive. We have made our decision to begin, and we take certain action toward an end. It is this movement that keeps us in touch with our humanness. True, there is a time for inaction, but when the time for action arises, let us leap into it with total purpose and excitement.

Affirmation

My action fully reflects my purpose.

June 6

Expansion

As we experience our power, we can feel ourselves expanding in our universe. We are not really growing but moving into full awareness of the Divinity within us. When we begin to become aware of our true breadth, we start letting go of fears and judgments, and appreciate life from a brand-new perspective.

Affirmation

I expand into my true self today.

June 7

Rhythm

There is probably no greater feeling of power than to be in the rhythm of life. Life has its rhythm, and when we allow ourselves to be gently in its beat everything works for us. The rhythm is the Love of God in action. If we are out of sorts, it is very helpful to remind ourselves that we merely have to let go of control and be in God's rhythm.

Affirmation

I am one with the rhythm of life today.

June 8

Realization

Gathering power unto ourselves, we come into the realization of who we are: loving children of God. The full realization of our worth follows, and life becomes a joy to experience. As we awaken to our own realization, we also are able to become aware of the fullness of everyone else we encounter every day of our life.

Affirmation

Today I realize totally who I am.

June 9

Excitement

We are excited when we tap into the power of the universe. Our energy sparkles and we are easily able to accomplish anything we wish. This excitement spills over to others, and we become a positive influence in their lives as well. Our connection with God deepens as our excitement for life increases.

Affirmation

My excitement for life increases moment by moment.

June 10
Caring

There is a great power in caring for ourselves and others. Our caring nature comes from Divine Love, and as we exercise it our spirit gains in strength. Life continues to increase in meaning as we care for our world. Caring for ourselves means seeing our real strength; caring for others means seeing the power in them.

Affirmation

I am powerful because I am caring.

June 11

Humor

When was the last time we found humor in the world, in ourselves? As we find humor in life's situations, we empower ourselves. When we don't take the world so seriously, we can travel life's path lightly. Humor gives us the power to deal with the most challenging of experiences in our lives and not be thrown off course.

Affirmation

My humor keeps me well-rounded.

June 12

Consistency

We demonstrate our power when we are consistent in life. The normal view of life is that it has its ups and downs, but it does not have to be that way. As we touch the God in us with more frequency, the bumps in life's road smooth out and we live from the center of our being. We attract what we want when we are consistent.

Affirmation

I live my life with consistency.

June 13

Faith

We have faith in ourselves; we have faith in others; but mostly we have faith in God. Our faith is our power of life. When we occasionally forget, we simply need to turn within and recontact with faith, which never wavers. Faith in the completeness of life through God sustains us in all situations in which we find ourselves.

Affirmation

My faith in God supports my life fully.

June 14

Beauty

Beauty truly is in the eye of the be-
holder. We see the power of beauty
in all things when we come from our
Divine place of observation. When
we drop opinions and judgments,
the beauty of everyone, of all situations becomes apparent to us. We
are also able to see the innate
beauty that exists throughout our
own beings.

Affirmation

I see the beauty of all things every
day.

June 15

Creativity

What a joy life is when we exercise the power of creativity. Even the most routine chores become fun when we cast a creative eye upon them. All creativity comes from God, and we can practice that creativity when we are in touch with the Divine. As we allow our creativity to be expressed, we automatically share it with others.

Affirmation

I am a creative child of God.

June 16

Personality

There is power in our personality, and it can be a positive or a negative power. To ensure that we come from our positive nature, we must turn to the God within. When we journey through our days displaying a positive personality that reflects our Divine nature, we have a glorious effect on ourselves and others.

Affirmation

My personality positively affects everyone I touch.

June 17

Body

We each possess a body traveling through this existence, and it reflects the power we direct through it. The body responds to our thoughts, obeys our every command. It reflects whatever is going on in our life. When we tenderly care for the body, we are demonstrating how we feel about life as well.

Affirmation

My body is a positive reflection of my life.

June 18
Touch

Physical touch is a powerful, loving method of expressing ourselves. From a handshake to a hug to love-making, we can express who we are to the world through touch. We need to remember to place the power of love behind every touch. Our physical contact then becomes a dynamic expression of who we are.

Affirmation

I touch everyone in love.

June 19

Voice

What we say is who we are. The power of our voice can literally shape our lives, from the home to the workplace to our recreation. We must be mindful when we speak, so that the words we utter come from a place of love. We can imagine that the power and presence of God is behind us every time we speak.

Affirmation

My voice affects everyone positively.

June 20

Vitality

If we dragged out of bed this morning, we are probably questioning our vitality. Vitality is a decision we make for power. We choose vitality, and when we do, our lives become full, interesting, and joyful. Our inner strength is limitless, and it is up to us to show this to the world through our vitality.

Affirmation

My vitality is powerful today and every day.

June 21

Pleasure

Pleasure is not bestowed upon us. It is something we create moment by moment. Any experience we have can be lived with pleasure. There is a boundless inner joy we can always access and apply to all situations, even challenging ones. When we add pleasure to life, we add power as well.

Affirmation

I experience all of life with pleasure.

June 22

Observation

There is a time for action and a time for observation. We often exercise more power in a circumstance by observing it than by doing something. To observe effectively, we come from a place of confidence and trust. After we observe completely, then is the time we can take action.

Affirmation

I am comfortable observing life.

June 23

Stillness

If we are caught up in the busy-ness of life, we can lose touch with who we are. A retreat into the stillness can immediately reconnect us. Meditation practiced daily helps us always remember our Source. All meaningful guidance in life comes from that Source and most often comes to us in the stillness.

Affirmation

I receive my guidance in the stillness.

June 24

Forgiveness

Everything happens in the now. It cannot happen in the past. The way we powerfully release the past is to forgive, forgive, forgive. Then we clear our minds and spirits to be the productive individuals we all are. Remember that there is never a problem in life that forgiveness cannot heal. When we truly forgive, we completely forget.

Affirmation

My life works perfectly because I forgive.

June 25

Knowing

Knowing is power. Knowing is the total confidence that all of life works smoothly. Knowing is our confidence in our God bond. When we study, pray, and meditate, knowing is the result. The awareness of our knowing occurs only in the present moment, so letting go of extraneous, petty thoughts is a key to reaching that state.

Affirmation

My knowing connects me with God.

June 26

Smiling

Smiling, à la the Mona Lisa, is a reflection of our inner peace. Looking at ourselves in the mirror and smiling can reinforce it for ourselves. Smiling gently at others lets them know we can be wholly trusted. The smile is a quiet reflection of power and a manifestation of the God within. When we smile, we are at peace.

Affirmation

Today I smile with love at everyone.

June 27

Love

Love is omnipotent and comes from God. The power of love is beyond anything we can imagine or have probably experienced. When we focus on love, the angels of the heavens gather to assist us in our journey. Love brings us the kind of peace nothing else can. Love is what we are. Love is who we are. Love is all-powerful. Love is.

Affirmation

I am total love today.

June 28

Innocence

Real power is innocent. Coming from a place of innocence, we come from a place not colored by the judgments of the world. We come from a place that offers unlimited possibilities in life. We come from a place in which manifestation is easy. We come from a place where love is all there is all the time.

Affirmation

My innocence offers me exactly what I want.

June 29

Reality

There is only one Reality, and it is God. The so-called realities of life are but our vain imaginings. When we connect with Reality, we connect with all that matters. Reality is all-powerful and all-pleasurable. It is up to us whether or not we stir around in the lower-case reality or whether we soar in the Reality of God.

Affirmation

Today I accept only Reality in my life.

June 30

Divinity

There is Divinity in everything. Its total power permeates every millisecond of our life with total love, joy, and peace. Life makes little sense to us when we come from our ego and total sense to us when we connect with its Divinity. It is important that we become still and connect with God as frequently throughout each day as possible.

Affirmation

I often turn to Divinity today.

July

Healing

July 1

Mind

Healing of the mind is really removing any blocks we have to Divine awareness. Our life exists because of and through our mind, and our mind exists in concert with Universal Mind. As we remove any impedance to the connection of our mind with Universal Mind, we heal ourselves on the most basic of levels.

Affirmation

My mind is healed today.

July 2

Body

Healing our body is loving our body and taking care of it. We are much more than just our bodies, but our bodies are our mirrors of how we view ourselves and all of life. When we lavish healing love on our bodies, we are living a healthy life. We look at ourselves in the mirror and we see the God stuff we are made of.

Affirmation

I always maintain a healthy body.

July 3

Spirit

Our spirit doesn't need healing, but as with our mind, we can get in the way of our connection with it. Regular prayer, meditation, and other spiritual work are the "healing" required for spirit. God knows we are perfection, and our spiritual path is our demonstration of this perfection.

Affirmation

Today I nurture my spirit in every way.

July 4

Others

Although it is up to other people ultimately to heal themselves, we can have a great part in their healing process by seeing them healed through our prayers. Our prayers always ask for their highest good; we need be no more specific than this. We practice unity when we share our healing power with our friends, relatives, and acquaintances.

Affirmation

I see the highest good for all people.

July 5

Workplace

If we ever have challenges in the workplace, on the job, or with others on the job, we can transform the situation by sending healing energy. We can start this day in the quiet by seeing harmony for ourselves and others in the workplace. When we begin a day with such positive thoughts, healing miracles will happen on the job.

Affirmation

My workplace is whole, happy, and healed.

July 6

Cause

The cause of a situation is the result of our mind-set. When we visualize upset, we create upset. When we visualize healing, we create healing. It is important we never underestimate our own powers of causation. An awareness of this power and a mind filled with healing thoughts will manifest harmony as we walk through life.

Affirmation

My thoughts of healing create harmony.

July 7

Perception

How we perceive a situation is how it is. We may see nothing but upset on the surface, but if we look for it we also can find healing existing at the same time. It is entirely up to us to see it healed. Remembering that we always have free will, we look for the healing in every instance and then we perceive it.

Affirmation

I perceive only healing today.

July 8

Influence

We influence ourselves and others every day, and we are influenced at the same time. If we come from a healed space, we effect healing in others and we are not changed by negative attitudes. Becoming aware of how much influence we possess is not ego. It is getting fully in contact with the Spirit of God, who works through us.

Affirmation

My healing influence is God-centered.

July 9

Attitude

Most of our attitudes were formed when we were children and came from parents or parent-figures. As we became adults, we embraced them as our own. We can blame others for our challenges, but if we take full responsibility for them we grow spiritually. Good health is a result of "owning" what is our own and changing it as we need to.

Affirmation

I have a healthy attitude and take full responsibility for my life.

July 10
Character

Our character is an intricate inter-
weaving of ideas and thoughts that
we have embraced throughout our
lives. The essence of our character is
what prompts our life decisions, and
a healthy character makes wise decisions. We can remind ourselves
daily that our character always
comes from a healed stance.

Affirmation

My character is totally healed.

July 11

Honesty

A healthy mind always tells the complete truth as quickly as possible, for there is never anything to hide. By always being honest we tremendously uncomplicate our lives, for we are never caught up in subterfuge. Honesty allows us to be totally who we are all the time. Our honesty represents the openness of God in us.

Affirmation

I always tell the absolute truth.

July 12

Abundance

Health and abundance are synonymous. When we are witness to the incredible abundance of life that surrounds us and which we move through every moment, we are indeed coming from a healthy place. The abundance we experience comes from God's Love, which is everywhere manifest. We just have to be open to see it.

Affirmation

Today I experience the abundance of God's Love.

203

July 13
Animals

The animal kingdom has become a human responsibility. Whether wild or domestic, animals depend on our protection for their survival. We serve them by visualizing their individual health and the health of entire species. Their health is yet another reflection of the way we feel about ourselves.

Affirmation

I visualize the survival and health of all animals.

July 14

Plants

> We control the plant kingdom and its health. Through our thoughts and actions, the health of all plants is the result of our consciousness. We despoil plants and ourselves when we recklessly do away with them or control them with chemicals instead of with caring. Our positive thoughts become positive prayers for plants.

Affirmation

> I take responsibility for the health of plants.

July 15

Environment

It is easy to understand how completely we are tied to the health of our environment. All we need to do is to see our environment with love and kindness the way we do our friends and family. We have an intrinsic symbiotic relationship with our environment. Our survival depends on it; its survival depends on us.

Affirmation

I live in harmony with the environment.

July 16

Order

> When our lives are in order, we are leading healthy lives. There is a natural order in all things from God. We do not have to be compulsive to have order in our lives. We simply have to allow that order to emerge from every idea, every possibility. Allowing order to direct us leads us to a state of healthy awareness.

Affirmation

> I allow order to emerge from every situation.

July 17

Imagination

What healthier activity than to get in touch with our imagination! Life is change, and our imagination is the tool we use to change joyfully. The creation of all newness on our planet comes from the healthy cultivation of a fertile imagination. As we live from our imagination, life becomes fuller and jam-packed with possibilities.

Affirmation

My healthy imagination directs me today.

July 18

Stillness

In the stillness, health is all there is. It is important to retreat from the noise of living to a quiet place in prayer or meditation to touch our innate healthiness. Stillness is nurturing, filling. We recharge our batteries in the stillness. We hear direction from the Voice for God in the stillness. We grow in the stillness.

Affirmation

I take time today for myself in the stillness.

July 19
Closeness

If we are feeling isolated, getting close to someone else is healing. If that is not practical, then talking to them on the phone works. If that can't be done, simply bring one you care about onto your mental screen and feel the connection. We come from Oneness, and being close to another reminds us of our loving Source.

Affirmation

I take time today to experience closeness with another.

July 20

Results

We achieve results in life through a healthy attitude. If we seem to be stuck in a project, with a goal we can take some time to look within and gently release any negative thoughts we may be experiencing. It is important to do this the instant we feel blocked. Positive results quickly occur as we feel and act healthy.

Affirmation

My healthy attitude produces healthy results.

July 21

Shelter

There are times when we need shelter from the storm. When these times occur, the healthy action is to turn to God and release all your challenges to Her. God is always our shelter. She will always protect us from the raging seas of our mind. We must allow Divine energy to keep us safe until we emerge once again into the bright sun.

Affirmation

God is my shelter and protection in every need.

July 22

Stimulus

If we find ourselves stuck in life, we may need a new stimulus. We can find Divine guidance in many places—directly through prayer and meditation, or indirectly through teachers, friends, or books. The healthy thing for us to remember is that we remain open to a new direction. Then we simply await the perfect stimulus.

Affirmation

I am open and ready for a new stimulus.

July 23
Kindness

Our healthiest attitude and action is kindness, to ourselves and others. We come from a healed place when we exhibit kindness in any form. Kindness expects nothing in return. It is its own reward. We also promote physical and mental healing when we engage in kind acts. Kindness is of God.

Affirmation

I invigorate myself through kindness today.

July 24

Interdependence

We are interdependent with others and with our universe—not in a codependent way but in a healthy way that lovingly announces: "I am one with you." Our nature is to interact and interrelate. As we do we become healthier, happier human beings who are living our purpose to the maximum.

Affirmation

I am one with everyone and everything.

July 25

Safety

We might think otherwise from time to time, but we are always safe. Our safety is guaranteed by God, and when we feel it we are healthy. If we feel fear, we must quickly turn within to our Source and affirm otherwise. Once we realize that nothing, including ourselves, dies, we will feel safe at all times.

Affirmation

I am safe in God.

July 26

Celebration

Our health calls for celebration today. In fact, when we celebrate we
ensure our good health on every
level. Seeing life as a continuous
celebration, we pronounce our innate fitness. When we celebrate our
good fortune, we automatically
touch everyone else in our life. Our
God nature calls for celebration.

Affirmation

I celebrate my perfect health today.

217

July 27

Accord

> We arise today in accord with the universe. All things this day flow easily and positively through us, and we connect with others every moment. The accord we feel comes from the Creator of all things, and all we have to do is let it bubble up through our being. We are in healthy accord, and we are one.

Affirmation

> I am in accord with all things.

July 28

Breath

Our breath is our life. When we breathe shallowly, we are usually in a state of challenge, fear, or ill health. When we take deep breaths, we affirm physically our Divine connection. Deep breathing is the essence of meditation and of moving our mind to our God center.

Affirmation

I breathe deeply the healthy breath of God today.

July 29

Vision

Our vision expands today and sees the perfect health of everyone. We know we are wondrously inter-related, and our vision confirms this. Our vision encompasses our entire being, not just our eyes, in "seeing" the truth in all people, things, and experiences. Our vision comes directly from God.

Affirmation

My vision witnesses complete healing.

July 30
World

A healed world is what we seek. We must embrace that goal in our every thought. Our every action must be directed toward that end. Our every word must come from a place of peace to ensure that a healing occurs. This healing is not a static event but an ongoing process that requires our continued vigilance to be realized.

Affirmation

Today I accept my part for the healing of the world.

July 31

Oneness

Our healing brings us to oneness: oneness with one another, oneness with God. The awareness of our oneness is our purpose in life. As we awaken to our oneness, life becomes a process of gentle flow. Life takes on a deep, loving meaning that guides us every moment of every day toward the peace that we ever seek.

Affirmation

I am healed by the awareness of my oneness.

AUGUST

Peace

August 1

Self

Peace is an inside job. Before there can be peace anywhere in our world, there has to be peace within us. We create peace in ourselves by being still each day, by quickly forgiving others and ourselves, by seeing peace in every circumstance of our life. The peace we discover in ourselves automatically extends to others.

Affirmation

I am at peace within myself.

August 2

Humanity

As we do personally, all of humankind craves peace. We support this yearning by visualizing peace for other individuals and the countries in which they live. We support this human desire by sharing our peacefulness with others in our home, our workplace, our nation. We support all peaceful activities of others.

Affirmation

I support all humanity in its quest for peace.

August 3

Receptivity

We are open and receptive to peace today and every day. That's how we come to live in a peaceful world. When we have a negative thought and we release it, we are announcing to the Universe that we are ready to receive peace now. The wonderful aspect of peace is that it always exists in us. We only have to be receptive to it.

Affirmation

I am receptive to peace today.

August 4

Communicating

If we find ourselves communicating with others in a less-than-peaceful fashion, a conscious altering of the words we use can assist us in changing our mind to peace. Our words carry much power in them, and when we select them carefully to reflect the peace we wish to convey, we lovingly serve ourselves and the world.

Affirmation

I communicate peace to all others today.

August 5

Listening

Our listening is selective. When we hear upset, we are upset. On the other hand, when we hear peace, we are peaceful. Our listening always echoes our consciousness. So when we hear other than peace, we need to be still for a moment, locate the thought that allows us to hear the upset, and release. Then we will hear only peace.

Affirmation

Today I hear only peace.

August 6

Learning

Even though peace is part of our makeup, we can learn about peace from the great teachers of the world and from our friends and relatives. We don't have to learn from a book or a classroom; we can learn just as easily from our daily interactions with others and through our powers of observation. When we open to learning, we are blessed.

Affirmation

I am open to learning more about peace.

August 7
Teaching

We always teach what we are. If we come from a place of upset, we teach upset. If we come from a place of peace, we teach peace. When we deal with others, it is helpful to remember we are the teacher. Then we are more apt to treat them with love, with kindness, with peace. From that posture we teach from our God-self.

Affirmation

I teach only peace.

August 8

Prosperity

Many of us think of prosperity as money, whereas true prosperity is a happy heart A happy heart is a heart at peace. When we are in fear, we feel lack. But when we are in peace, we feel full and prosperous. We walk in the woods, sit in the stillness, and feel the peacefulness around us. We are then in touch with true prosperity.

Affirmation

My peacefulness brings me prosperity.

August 9

Goodness

When we think of goodness, we very often think of doing good deeds. That is valid, because good deeds are a correction from upset to peace. But being at peace is in and of itself goodness. We needn't do anything to be at peace. When we get in touch with peace, we get in touch with the goodness at the core of our heart.

Affirmation

My goodness brings me peace.

August 10

Usefulness

If we struggle with our purpose in life and feel less than useful, it is valuable to take time to reconnect with the peaceful processes ever bubbling within us. We are never more useful than when we live life through our peaceful center. A few moments apart from our world, and we can sit in the quiet and join with our peaceful usefulness.

Affirmation

I am useful because I am at peace.

August 11

Willingness

Our willingness to see the universe as a peaceful place is all it takes to change our lives from chaos to quiet. That willingness announces to God that we are ready for any peaceful alterations to our nature that are necessary. Our being willing for the new in our lives means we are prepared to live a happy life from this moment on.

Affirmation

I am willing to allow peace in my life.

August 12
Practice

Like playing the piano or riding a bicycle, peace takes practice. Most of us were raised with many less-than-peaceful messages, which we became used to. It takes an active awareness to change our consciousness permanently to peace. We must practice every day to release upset and replace it with peace. Practice *does* make perfect.

Affirmation

I practice peace today.

August 13
Meditation

Peace lives in us all the time. A daily routine of meditation, preferably at the beginning of each day, takes us to the center of our being, where peace lives. In Western society, meditation can be a challenge, since we think we have to be doing something every moment. Meditation is doing nothing—peace.

Affirmation

As I meditate, I experience peace.

August 14

Loving

Love and peace coexist. Love is peace. We cannot love if we are in a state of upset or agitation. When we share love with our spouse, our family, our friends, our partners at work, we are sharing peace. Our loving nature expressed is what will ultimately bring peace to our world. Our loving peace comes from God.

Affirmation

My peacefulness expresses as love today.

August 15

Sharing

We cannot keep peace to ourselves. As we place ourselves in a peaceful state of mind, we automatically share our peace with others. As we extend to others, our peace grows, their peace grows, and peace in the world grows. Sharing the Divine peace that lives within us is perhaps our most important function on this planet.

Affirmation

I share peace with everyone.

August 16

Worship

As we worship God in the way of our choosing, we are announcing that peace is the most important aspect of our lives. God is silent. Peace is silent. But worship points the action of our thoughts lovingly toward God and peace. The next time we engage in our form of worship, we may choose to unite the thoughts of God and peace.

Affirmation

My worship leads me to peace.

August 17
Wisdom

We express the wisdom of the ages when we express peace. Our decision-making process is not necessarily wise unless every decision is one that arises from the peaceful center of our being. Wisdom is knowing how to incorporate peace in every decision, every area of our lives. When we are wise, we are at peace.

Affirmation

I am wise; therefore I am at peace.

August 18

Awe

If we stand in awe of God, we stand in awe of peace. Our being in awe allows us to place peace in its true perspective as the true essence of everything that has been, is, or will be. Peace stands as a mighty, silent tribute to God. And as we stand in awe of the magnificence of peace, we connect with the omnipotence of God.

Affirmation

Today I stand in awe of peace.

August 19

Moment

We cannot have peace in the past;
we cannot have peace in the future.
Peace can exist only in the moment.
To ensure a possibility of peace in
the future, it is imperative that we
practice it this moment, every moment of every day. By bringing our
minds back to peace each moment,
we are doing everything we need to
live life to its utmost.

Affirmation

I have peace in this moment.

August 20

Giving

What greater gift can we give than peace! We give it in a thought, a look, a word, a pose, a touch. We give peace with every kind thought we have about anyone or any circumstance. When we give peace, the Universe expands a little more. When we give peace, we stay in contact with the stuff of God. Giving peace is everything.

Affirmation

I generously give peace today.

August 21
Skill

Peace is a skill, but it is not one we learn. We awaken to it, since it is one we are born with. If we forget it for a time, we remember we can always consciously choose peace over any upsetting circumstance by practicing peace each day of our lives. It is a skill to live peacefully every moment of the day.

Affirmation

I awaken to the skill of peace.

August 22

Approval

We live in peace, and we attract the approval of the world. We extend peace, and our approval comes from heaven. Peace is its own approval. As we live peacefully, we give approval to everyone we meet also to maintain a peaceful countenance. They in turn similarly touch others, and peace expands by the moment.

Affirmation

My approval comes from my peaceful center.

August 23

Beauty

We see the beauty in a loved one.
We see the beauty of a sunset. We
see the beauty of our beloved pet.
We see the beauty of ourselves.
When we see such beauty, we are
seeing the peace that lives in all
things shining through. The real
beauty of peace is that it is everywhere present in all things at all
times.

Affirmation

The beauty of peace is all I see.

August 24

Friendliness

The friendliness we extend to others arises from our place of peace. The whole idea of friendship is one that is based on peace. We are not being an effective friend if we come from upset, if we come from insecurity. True friendliness is actually peace reaching out to touch another. Let us remember to share peace with our friends.

Affirmation

I express peace today through friendliness.

August 25

Recurring

We know we are living from our peaceful center when thoughts of peace are recurring. Also, recurring peaceful encounters become the norm for us rather than the exception. A repeating pattern of peace builds on itself, and we become more and more comfortable with living peace in every situation. Peace happens.

Affirmation

Peace is recurring in my life.

August 26

Flow

The flow of the Universe is peace. When we live in the flow, we are peaceful. When we face an inordinate number of challenges, it means we are swimming against the flow. Peace is like a river, and we can live peace by allowing its flow to carry us along. As we are in the flow, so are all the others we touch on our journey.

Affirmation

I live in the flow of peace.

August 27

Deserving

When life presents numerous challenges, we may question our deservability. Peace, however, never questions it. When we are in a peaceful state, we know we are deserving of that peace. We know we are in the natural state that always expresses peace and always receives peace as a Universal right.

Affirmation

I deserve peace.

August 28

Rejoicing

We have discovered that peaceful place within us, and it is completely appropriate that we rejoice in it. As we rejoice in our peace, we reinforce it. As we rejoice in our peace, we extend it to the world. As we rejoice in our peace, we live from a place of perfection. Our rejoicing is the cement holding peace in its place in our center.

Affirmation

I rejoice in my peacefulness today.

August 29
Mind

Our mind is filled with thoughts, and sometimes too many of these thoughts confuse us. To rectify that dilemma, we simply need to replace all thoughts with one—peace. This is not a onetime process. It is ongoing, as we replace fear with peace, upset with peace, sadness with peace. Our peaceful mind becomes a very powerful mind indeed.

Affirmation

My mind is filled with the thought of peace.

August 30

Global

As we fill ourselves with peace, we extend it to the world. Peace on a global scale must come from the peace process within each individual world citizen. If we can start wars, we can start peace. We must fill ourselves with the knowing that our peace is effecting global peace. Our peaceful thoughts and actions create the world's peace.

Affirmation

Today I extend my peace globally.

August 31

God

The Peace of God is all there is.
When we experience other than this
peace, it is coming from our ego.
The Peace of God is eternal. All
other feelings we experience are
temporal. We were created out of
the Peace of God. Our purpose in
being is to rediscover this Peace
within us which has never left us
and will exist forever.

Affirmation

I experience the Peace of God today.

September

Fulfillment

September 1

Individuality

We seem to live in this world as individuals expressing unique personalities. When we accept this role, our next step is to fulfill ourselves physically, mentally, and spiritually. Our fulfillment is the primary reason we arose this morning, so this day and every day it is important to take steps toward our personal completion.

Affirmation

All I do this day moves me toward fulfillment.

September 2

Feeling

Our feeling nature is what we tap into as we sense how unlimited we are. Feelings aren't to be confused with emotions. Emotions come from our ego. Feelings come from our God connection and our measure of aliveness. We use our thinking nature as we acquire facts, while our feeling nature is used to obtain universal knowledge.

Affirmation

I attune myself to my true feelings.

September 3

Knowledge

An awareness of the universal knowledge of everything leads us to fulfillment. Sound imposing? Not when we become aware that all knowledge is within us, and all we need do is make contact with it. As the light of knowledge illumines us, we move closer and closer to complete fulfillment.

Affirmation

The light of knowledge illumines my mind today.

September 4

Artistic

Our artistic side must *be* in order for us to complete ourselves. We all have an artistic bent longing to emerge. Whether it be painting, music, model building, origami, it makes no difference. It must be expressed. We need to give ourselves time in every day or at least every week to allow this artistic expression to manifest.

Affirmation

Today I allow my artistic talents to complete me.

September 5

Job

"Job fulfillment" has become almost a cliché, but it doesn't have to be. If we will look at our jobs as part of an integrated life we are leading, fulfillment there is as important as in any other area in our lives. We come from our God space and love what we are doing on the job, so that we will always be in a place of discovering fulfillment.

Affirmation

My job always fulfills me.

September 6

Leisure

Leisure time has much more importance than we give it credit for. If we are steadily achieving our goals and still are not being fulfilled, it is probably because we are not giving ourselves enough time to sit and just be. Leisure is important for recharging our batteries. We will be surprised at how full we can feel by just allowing ourselves idle time.

Affirmation

I allow myself plenty of leisure time.

September 7

Travel

When we take a trip, personal or business, or just travel to the grocery store, we need to be aware of our environment and drink it in. When we do, we round ourselves out. If our physical movements from place to place are done with mental blinders on, we miss out on much of the joy of life and slow our fulfillment to a snail's pace.

Affirmation

I fulfill myself through travel.

September 8

Giving

Our life is going as we want it to, and yet we are still not feeling fulfilled. Giving of our time, our talents, our treasures may be the answer. When we give, we announce to the Universe that we are living in an abundant world and that our fulfillment is everyone's fulfillment. Sharing with others is always completing ourselves.

Affirmation

Today I complete myself by giving to others.

September 9

Connecting

We do not lead an isolated life, and it is important that we connect personally with our fellow human-kind. As we do, we experience the Oneness of God in our life, and with that Oneness comes fulfill-ment. A smile or a kind word to a stranger we encounter on the street is often enough for us to feel that connection.

Affirmation

I fulfill myself today as I connect with others.

September 10

Openness

We are open and willing to receive all that life has to offer, and the result is a feeling of total fulfillment. If we remember that we are not in charge and God is, we open ourselves to learning life's lessons gently rather than with a struggle. A quiet time of prayer or meditation at the beginning of each day is all we need to open ourselves.

Affirmation

Today I take time to open to all of life.

September 11

Synchronicity

There is a synchronicity in all of life
that, when we connect with it, leads
to our own fulfillment. Life moves
at a Divine pace, which is always
there for us to discover. It is like
grabbing the strap on a subway car
and holding on. We have to do little
other than be aware that it exists.
We let go and let God.

Affirmation

I am one with the flow of life.

September 12

Activity

> We've prayed and meditated, and
> now it's time for us to engage in the
> activity of our choice to reach fulfill-
> ment. Whatever activity we select
> is perfect if we allow the Voice for
> God to direct our every move. Aim-
> less action is frustrating, but Di-
> vine right action is the result of our
> listening to our clear direction.

Affirmation

> Divine right action guides and ful-
> fills me today.

September 13

Maturity

We grow from children into adults,
but that does not guarantee fulfillment. True maturity is spiritual and
comes when we open ourselves to
God. We embrace even the unpleasant in our lives, for we know it is all
lessons for us to learn. We know we
are maturing spiritually when our
life feels complete every moment of
the day.

Affirmation

I am spiritually mature and complete.

September 14

Support

> Our world is a mutual support
> system. Every element of Mother
> Earth is mutually supportive of
> every other element. Of course, we
> can block that flow and often do,
> but when we allow it we live in ful-
> fillment. It is vital that we support
> other people and our total environ-
> ment, and as we do, we are sup-
> ported fully in return.

Affirmation

> As I support my world, I am ful-
> filled.

September 15

Wonder

If we become the child in our view of life and see it in wonder, we are adding another building block to our fulfillment. Our routines often block our vision, so that we miss much of the daily wonder that is there for our beholding. The next time we look out the window of our home or car, we can embrace all we see in newness and wonder.

Affirmation

I am always aware of the wonder in my midst.

September 16

Goals

Goals are necessary for us to achieve fulfillment. When we set a goal, we lovingly nudge ourselves into thought and action that make our life more well-rounded. Our goals are dynamic and can be changed at any time, but their existence is needed for us to feel we are moving toward completion. We can see goals as the flow of God.

Affirmation

Today I move toward fulfilling my goals.

September 17

Existence

When we look at who we are, we may question our existence or we may marvel at it. But if we will be open to its totality, we move one step closer to personal fulfillment. The "I" in our existence is that part of us that can observe and experience the all-ness of our universe. It is helpful to thank God daily for our existence.

Affirmation

Thank you, God, for the gift of life.

September 18

Unity

As we feel unity with others and our world, we feel fulfilled indeed. We do not exist as an island on a sea, but rather as a drop of water in that sea that is at once unique to and one with the entire vastness of the great body of water. If we feel separate, we are coming out of our ego. On the other hand, our unity comes from God.

Affirmation

I affirm my unity with all, and I am fulfilled.

September 19

Trust

We trust in one another, and we trust in God. As we do, we feel complete as human beings. Trust is the natural order of everything. Mistrust was created by human fear. To trust is to have faith in a Supreme Creator and to have faith that all of life, not just selected portions of it, is meaningful. As we trust, we grow.

Affirmation

Today I am fulfilled because I trust.

September 20

Excellence

In all we think and do, if we strive
for excellence we will feel complete.
Excellence is the state of seeing the
Divinity in anything. Excellence
leads us to more excellence, so our
seeing it moment by moment in life
keeps us connected to our Source.
When we live in excellence, we live
in wholeness.

Affirmation

I live my life in a state of excellence.

September 21

Truth

When we live a life of fulfillment, we live a life of truth. Truth on every level is necessary. We must always tell the truth. We must always connect with the truth of existence. We must always be open to the Truth of God. As we live a life of truth, we know we are on purpose. Truth is definitely the only way.

Affirmation

Truth fulfills me today.

September 22

Life

Life is everything in our awareness.
It is the fullness of our expression. It
is what we experience within every
fiber of our being. We can watch life,
or we can live life. When we live life,
we are fulfilled. Life is the joy of
the sun, of a touch, of a ripe piece
of fruit, of dancing, of laughing, of
swimming, of flying . . . of being.

Affirmation

I embrace life totally.

September 23

Grace

When we are in a state of grace, we are truly in the flow of everything good. Grace then becomes our fulfillment. Grace emanates from God, though we have complete free will either to accept or reject it. Even if we are unaware of the feeling of grace, all we need do is live as though grace were our natural state of being.

Affirmation

I live in a state of grace.

September 24

Gentleness

Living gently is the way we experience life at its most nurturing. We need to be gentle with ourselves, with others, with our environment. As we come more and more from a gentle space, we receive gentleness in kind from every situation. It is simple to share gentleness, for that is our basic nature.

Affirmation

Today I express my gentleness.

September 25

Healing

We are whole beings, but we have gained misinformation through the years which hasn't served us. So many of us have the appearance of needing healing. To be truly healed we need to reconnect with our inner wholeness through prayer and meditation. As we make new contact with our healed self, we realize our fulfillment.

Affirmation

My body is whole, well, and strong.

September 26

Peace

> We have peace like a river in our souls. Let us today look at the world and all its components with a wholly peaceful vision. Our peacefulness is so fulfilling, and its wonderful part is that it can be shared with everyone. Our peace stems from our God-self and is the way the universe was created. Chaos is illusion. Peace is reality.

Affirmation

> I share peace with everyone today.

September 27

Joy

Sometimes we awaken feeling blue. When that happens, we just need to realize that our ego was the first to awaken this morning. We must gently nudge our ego out and allow the spirit, which is pure joy, into awareness. A brief meditation, a quick prayer will do this. When we travel through the day in joy, we do so as fulfilled individuals.

Affirmation

I allow joy to complete me.

September 28

Loving

Loving is the most wonderful aspect of life. We know we are whole beings when we love ourselves, love others, love all facets of our universe. Love is the stuff of God that fills us every moment. Love holds our very existence together, keeping us near to the bosom of our Creator. Let us all love fully and unconditionally all the time.

Affirmation

I fill myself with love today.

September 29

Planetary

The fulfillment of our planet arises from our personal fulfillment. Our planet is made complete through our caring and love. God is the creator, but we are the caretakers. And we can fulfill our functions perfectly by nurturing our home in the tenderest of ways. We all have a part to fill in keeping Mother Earth vital and supportive.

Affirmation

Today I help fulfill Mother Earth.

September 30

Spiritual

> We are here to fulfill ourselves
> spiritually. Let us all nurture our
> spiritual disciplines of praying,
> meditating, loving, being kind, tak-
> ing responsibility, commitment. As
> we move toward spiritual comple-
> tion, there is no other aspect of life
> that need concern us. We turn to-
> ward God this day and give thanks
> for our spiritual growth.

Affirmation

> I thank God for life and fulfillment.

O CTOBER

Wisdom

October 1

Expansion

As we sail through our time of life, we open ourselves to an ever-expanding world of input and information. We need to use wisdom to select and filter the items that serve us and release those that don't. The perfect technique to accomplish this is to continually ask for the guidance of God and open ourselves to His Wisdom.

Affirmation

The Wisdom of God is expanding me now.

October 2

Feelings

Our feelings are who we are, and when we use our feelings wisely life flows smoothly for us. When we use wisdom we will take an appropriate amount of time to respond to a situation rather than acting rashly. Our feelings reflect the vibrancy of life, and our wisdom keeps our feelings serving us in a positive manner.

Affirmation

My feelings always reflect my highest good.

October 3

Bonding

The wise among us are aware of our bond with all of life. We connect with its Divinity and feel the oneness which is the reality of everything. We bond with other people almost daily, and our wisdom prevents us from doing so indiscriminately. The bonding we do helps move us to become whole human beings.

Affirmation

Today I wisely bond with all of life.

October 4

Trust

If we have problems trusting others, we must look to our own trust-worthiness. Do we feel we are in charge, or do we feel God is in charge? When we use wisdom, we trust God, we trust ourselves, and we trust others. Perhaps the biggest step we can take is to relinquish control of life and know that God will take care of everything.

Affirmation

I trust in God's infinite Wisdom.

October 5

Positiveness

When we are beset with challenges of negativity, we are not using wisdom. Life works when we are positive; it doesn't when we are negative. Our wisdom allows us to see beyond limitations to the inherent positiveness in every encounter, indeed in all of life. We simply have to remember that being positive is always our choice.

Affirmation

I see the positive effects within every situation today.

October 6

Comfort

If we wonder whether or not we are living life with wisdom, we only need to look at our comfort level. If our decisions make us feel ill at ease, then perhaps we are acting without much forethought. As we wisely make decisions that confront us moment by moment, we feel completely relaxed and at peace with everything

Affirmation

I am comfortable with all of my life.

October 7

Agreement

Are we in disagreement with our
partner, our parent, our boss, the
next-door neighbor? If so, we are
probably not using wisdom. Agree-
ment in life's occurrences comes
from making wise choices, choices
that come from Universal Wisdom
and not from our ego. We simply
need to make each choice from the
God within us all.

Affirmation

Today all situations are agreeable.

October 8
Caring

A reality check we can use is to look at how self-centered we are at any time. If we are thinking mostly of ourselves and not of others, we need to alter that stance to one of caring. Our caring nature emanates from the wisdom that resides within, for as we care we acknowledge that we are one with all living beings.

Affirmation

In wisdom I care for all others to-day.

October 9

Safety

Are we safe? Always. Since we never leave the eternalness of God, we are always one with Him and therefore are always safe. We must tap into our God wisdom to know this, however. Our ego tells us that there is danger lurking out there. But the Spirit in us always assures us that we are ever living in complete safety.

Affirmation

I am always safe in the arms of God.

October 10

Peace

Peace is synonymous with wisdom. When we are in a quiet state, a prayerful state, a meditative state, we come to peace from a place of wisdom. We always know if we are acting wisely by examining just how peaceful we feel. If we detect agitation, we simply bring our self back to center through our spiritual practice.

Affirmation

My wisdom always gives me peace.

October 11

Seeing

As we allow wisdom to flow through us more every day, our seeing the fullness of life and its joys likewise increases. We do not have to change any aspect of our being to increase our seeing. We merely have to listen to the wise voice within that is always directing us. We release control . . . we allow . . . we see.

Affirmation

Today I see the fullness of life.

October 12

Unity

There is unity in everything, and as we experience it we experience the deep wisdom of our being, which is an integral part of that unity. We always feel like a whole being when we experience unity. If we are feeling incomplete, we must gently bring ourselves back to that oneness. Our feeling of unity is our feeling of the Divine.

Affirmation

I feel unity with everyone today.

October 13

Attraction

We can attract all that is good in life to us every moment of every day, but we need to use wisdom in the process. With wisdom we share and send out that which we wish to attract. When we send peace, we attract peace. When we share joy, we attract joy. When we give love, we attract love.

Affirmation

Today I send out what I wish to attract.

October 14

Learning

> We learn all the time. Being selec-
> tive in what we learn is wisdom. As
> we grow spiritually, we gain in the
> Divinely inspired wisdom that we
> need to learn the wonderful lessons
> of life rather than the painful ones.
> When we take time to connect with
> our Higher Power, we always learn
> the valuable lessons.

Affirmation

> I always learn through wisdom.

October 15

Observation

Observing life on a deep level before we act is wisdom. We can be either a casual observer or a devoted observer. Our observation needs to be nonjudgmental, merely seeing things as they are, not deciding whether they are right or wrong. Using the power of our observation wisely vastly increases the scope of our lives.

Affirmation

I am a wise observer of life.

October 16

Decisions

The decisions we make in life are countless. If we make them with wisdom, our life works. If we make them haphazardly, life can be iffy. The decision-making process employed wisely gives our life a completeness it otherwise would lack. When in doubt about decisions, we turn them over to the Wisdom of the Divine.

Affirmation

Today I make all decisions with wisdom.

October 17

Harmony

As we are in the flow of life, we experience harmony in all things. If life loses its harmony, it is important that we look to our inner wisdom for correction. Harmony for us means our life flows effortlessly, all our relationships are loving, all our situations are joyous. Living in harmony means living in the natural order of things.

Affirmation

I experience harmony in every area of my life.

October 18

Love

All the wisdom of the Universe stems from love. We love ourselves; we love others; we love our planet. We give love and we receive love. The more we are in the tempo of love, the more we are connected to God. Love is the reason for every goal, the purpose behind every life. The more we love, the wiser we are.

Affirmation

I love totally through the Wisdom of God.

October 19
Awe

As we stand in awe of God and life, we open ourselves to experiencing the wisdom of the Universe. Awe is the trait of a child that, if we nurture it through life, will keep the world and all its experiences fresh for us. When we are in awe, we are able to see the Divine in everything. When we are in awe, life's meaning expands.

Affirmation

Today I stand in awe of my world.

October 20

Change

When we resist change, life is a struggle. When we embrace change, we are in tune with God's wisdom. Life is all about change, and when we allow change, we allow personal and spiritual growth. Allowing change allows us to fully experience the breadth of life. Our destiny is one of change.

Affirmation

I embrace change in my life today.

October 21

Happiness

We choose to be happy; we choose
to be unhappy. We may as well
choose happiness, for that is the
essence of who we are. When we decide for happiness, that is also the
choice for wisdom. Happiness is in-
fectious. Our smiles help others to
smile. Our laughter brings laughter
to others. Our joy elates others.

Affirmation

Today I choose happiness.

October 22
Sharing

If we are feeling lack in our lives, we can share something with another to experience prosperity. We share love, money, time, a meal, a movie, an idea, a hug. We come from a place of universal wisdom when we share. We acknowledge that our Universe is a wholly abundant place and that we are an instrument of that abundance.

Affirmation

I openly share with others today.

October 23

Forgiveness

Forgiveness is necessary for us to realize that we are really children of
God. True forgiveness acknowl-
edges God's Wisdom in a personal
way. We proclaim that there was
actually nothing to forgive after all,
that we simply changed our minds
and forgot totally about what is
was we were forgiving. That is true
wisdom.

Affirmation

I forgive and I totally forget.

October 24

Release

Holding on to anything, whether we see it as good or bad, slows down our spiritual growth. Wisdom is the realization that release leads to our individual advancement. Nothing is ours to own. It all comes from God, and we are merely the vehicles through which all of creation flows. When we practice release, we are in the flow.

Affirmation

Today I release my hold on everything.

October 25

Sureness

Wisdom is sureness. To be certain of something is not smugness if that sureness comes from the God within. When we are spiritually sure, we are in a loving space that doesn't have to be "right." We simply know that God is in charge and that we have the free will to live our life in accord with Divine flow.

Affirmation

Through God I am sure today.

October 26
Celebration

The Wisdom of Everything created a party atmosphere, which is always welcoming us to join in the celebration if we will. When we live life as a celebration, we are living it to the fullest. As we do, we engage others to join in the festivities. The music of life always plays for us, so we might as well join the orchestra.

Affirmation

My life is a celebration.

October 27

Vitality

If we are feeling listless and lackluster, we are off center and missing our natural inheritance of vitality. As we reconnect with the Wisdom of God, we get in touch once again with our vitality. Our mental and physical energy level is an easy indicator as to how well we are doing in our spiritual life. Our vitality is our connectedness.

Affirmation

I am overflowing with the vitality of God.

October 28

Truth

The truth of our lives is that we are children of a Divine Creator. That truth leads us to wisdom in every area of our life. We all have an individual divinity that is united with the One, and the awareness of that truth gives meaning to life. Connecting with truth is the only purpose we will ever need.

Affirmation

Today I connect with the truth of my being.

October 29

Contentment

If we arose this morning and meditated and connected with God, chances are we are spending the rest of the day in a state of contentment. All we need realize is that all our wants and desires are really a wish to return to God. When we discover or rediscover that fact, our life becomes one with the wisdom of contentment.

Affirmation

I am content because I am one with God.

October 30

Completion

> We crave completion, not realizing
> we are already complete in the eyes
> of God. True wisdom is knowing
> that we are complete just the way
> we are. We may have outer facets
> we wish to change, but our inner
> self is already one with God. When
> this moves into our awareness, we
> become effective teachers of God.

Affirmation

> Today I embrace my completion.

October 31

God

The final and only authority on wisdom is God. God's Wisdom is all there is. As we journey through life and connect with this Wisdom, we live full and complete existences. Our only required action is that we let go and let God in every situation. Life works for us as we connect with the only true Wisdom.

Affirmation

I turn my life over to the Wisdom of God.

November

Abundance

November 1
Personal

We are filled with an abundance
of all things required to make us
personally complete. As we acknowledge our personal abundance
overflowing, we sense a totality of
the self that indicates our real connection with our Creator. It is that
abundance that makes our life truly
worth living and gives us unparal-
leled contentment.

Affirmation

My abundance is complete today.

November 2

Family

When we look adoringly on our spouse, our parents, our children, our grandchildren, we awaken to the abundance that is inherent in the family unit. Our connection to family is needed for our world to succeed on its healing path. Most healing begins within the family, and an ever-expanding abundance is the result of that healing.

Affirmation

My family is my true abundance.

November 3

Workplace

Whether our jobs are within the home or at outside workplaces, they represent the universal abundance. We are the ones who must see and experience the abundance the workplace contains. Our co-workers are a major part of that abundance. When we integrate our jobs into the rest of our lives, we feel more totally abundant.

Affirmation

I experience abundance at my workplace today.

November 4

Nature

As we look out of a window, we see the wonder and fullness of nature. As we walk down the street or through the forest, we drink in the magnificence of the abundance of our outside environment. We can gain a real appreciation for the totality of life at any time by focusing our attention on nature.

Affirmation

I experience total abundance in nature.

November 5

Strength

We practice various kinds of strength: spiritual strength, physical strength, mental strength, loving strength, strength of purpose. All represent the abundance of who we are. True strength is God-connected in that it is always used for the good of ourselves and others. Using our strength wisely can lead us to completion.

Affirmation

I gather all my strength from God.

November 6

Success

We all strive for success of one kind or another. True success stems from the God within and fills us. Ego-based success leaves us with a feeling of always wanting more, always feeling incomplete. Success from our inner Divinity gives us a deep, abundant satisfaction and is readily shared with all those we know and love.

Affirmation

Today I feel the abundance of my success.

November 7
Movement

Living a static life with no change
gives us a sense of emptiness. But
if we allow for movement in all
areas of our life, we connect with
our abundance. The movement of
change is necessary for our spiritual
growth and puts us in touch with
who we really are. If we fear change,
creating some movement in our area
of fear will redirect us.

Affirmation

I welcome movement in my life today.

November 8

Creativity

As we connect with our creative spirit, what a wonderful feeling of abundance we experience! Whether we are creating on the job, in the kitchen, on a canvas, in our relationships, we feel the wonder of the Universe pouring through in every moment of the creative process. Our creativity comes from the God within us all.

Affirmation

Today I connect with the abundance of creativity.

November 9
Purpose

If we drift through life aimlessly, without purpose, we feel empty. But when we are filled with purpose, our life becomes one of total abundance. Our purpose is the fuel that motivates us moment by moment. When we move in alignment with our purpose, we move in concert with God. With purpose we lead a joyous life.

Affirmation

I discover my purpose today.

November 10
Vitality

> We are filled with the vitality of life, thus we are filled with abundance. Although it sometimes seems otherwise, our vitality is a choice we make every day. The creative power of the universe always flows through us, but if we choose to block that flow we limit our vitality. When we feel less than vital, we only have to remember God.

Affirmation

> I am vitally alive.

November 11

Joyfulness

As we connect with our joy, we understand the true meaning of abundance. Our joyfulness puts all challenges we face in proper perspective. Our joyfulness keeps us living life completely. Our joyfulness attracts to us the other joyful people in the universe. Sharing our joyfulness merely increases our own joyous spirit.

Affirmation

This day I become and remain joyful.

November 12

Timing

There is always the perfect time for anything to be accomplished. As we live in the Divine flow of abundance, our timing is impeccable. When we seem to be out of sync, we need to connect again to the God within in order to return the Divine flow. Prayer and meditation are the keys for this uniting with our inner timing device.

Affirmation

Today my timing is perfect in all matters.

November 13
Financial

Abundance is much more than money, but our financial state can be a clear indicator of just how fully we are living the abundant life. Money reflects our consciousness. When whatever we have is enough, we are living in abundance. When there is never enough, we need to correct our thinking so our finances go from frustration to fun.

Affirmation

My financial abundance overflows today.

November 14

Physical

Our health represents abundance that we manifest on the physical plane. When we are healthy, we are living in the flow of abundance. If we block the flow, our physical condition suffers. As we regularly forgive and release guilt, our physical state returns to natural perfect health. We must always remember the spirit-mind-body connection.

Affirmation

I always manifest perfect health.

November 15

Light

> The Light of God surrounds us all
> the time, enveloping us in the light
> of love, the light of wisdom, the
> light of understanding, the light of
> joy, the light of forgiveness, and the
> light of peace. We are the one who
> makes the choice to "see" the light.
> When we do, our life becomes one of
> incredible abundance.

Affirmation

> I live fully in the Light of God.

November 16

Wisdom

The wisdom we use to make life's decisions comes from the abundance of the Universe. If we are using wisdom, we do not always have to be right. Wisdom is seeing the good for everyone in every situation. True wisdom comes not from our intellect but from our feeling nature, which is joined with the full expanse of life.

Affirmation

Today all my decisions are made from wisdom.

November 17

Growth

The abundance of growth is joyfully witnessing our self expanding into Universal Consciousness. We are one with all things, and we are complete as we are. But what we understand as growth is our ever-increasing awareness of that oneness, that completeness. We experience daily growth as we connect with God.

Affirmation

I relish in my growth in consciousness today.

November 18

Harmony

Every person, every tree, every animal, every living thing interacts with every other living thing. The synergy of these relationships produces a natural harmony. We can either live with ease in the harmony, or we can elect to block it. If we choose the harmonious life, we live fully in God's abundance.

Affirmation

I live in harmony with all living things.

November 19

Beauty

We notice the beauty in a new life,
say in a kitten. We cradle the tiny
life in our hands, and we are replete
with the abundance of God's
beauty manifesting. Everything in
our world is inherently filled with
beauty. Our ideas and actions are
what make anything seem less than
beautiful. It is up to us to choose
beauty in our life.

Affirmation

Today I experience the beauty in all
of life.

November 20

Feeling

Our feelings give us that wondrous sense of utter aliveness, of living in a universe that is everywhere abundant. Our feeling nature stems from God. Through it flow love, compassion, joy, serenity. When we turn to our feeling nature, we open ourselves to everything positive, exciting, and Godlike that is ours to embrace.

Affirmation

I embrace all of my feelings today.

November 21

Completion

> We are complete just the way we are, but if we are living a life of struggle we have not connected with that truth. We have the freedom to make up our world the way we want to and then live it exactly in that manner. When we do, we practice living as whole, complete human beings and life fills us with meaning.

Affirmation

> I live my life as a complete human being.

November 22

Activity

We can go to a movie today, go to the park, go to work and accomplish much, go visit a friend. Or we can read a book, write a letter, sit in meditation. If our activity, whatever it is, has a loving purpose behind it, it will fill us with a feeling of abundance. We can allow any activity in which we engage to come from God.

Affirmation

All my activities today are God-directed.

November 23

Serenity

As we sit in stillness, we experience serenity. Serenity is not emptiness. On the contrary, sitting in the serenity of meditation can fill us with the feeling of abundance more than anything we do in our world. When we feel serenity, we open ourselves up to hearing the constant flow of loving messages that come from God.

Affirmation

I sit in serenity and feel the abundance of God.

November 24

Discovery

If we ever feel boredom with who we are, what we are doing, we simply must get off our derrieres and move into a discovery mode. That means moving into a place where you return to the child within, whose very purpose is and has always been discovering the newness in everything. What we discover is our abundance.

Affirmation

I am open to the discovery of all things new today.

November 25

Pleasure

Everywhere we turn there is pleasure. There is the pleasure of a sun-
rise, followed by the pleasure of a
delicious breakfast, followed by the
pleasure of the shower, followed by
countless pleasures throughout the
day. Every day when we arise, all
we have to do is look for the pleasures in life and we will find them in
all their abundance.

Affirmation

I seek and find all the pleasure of
life.

November 26

Forgiveness

We really understand the abundance of love we have within us when we can forgive others easily. The same awareness of love occurs as we forgive ourselves. What forgiveness does for us is to affirm that what needed forgiving was important only because it continually affected our lives. After forgiveness it is totally forgotten.

Affirmation

The abundance of my love comes from forgiveness.

345

November 27

Life

The nature of life is abundance.
When we fully connect with our
aliveness, we are in touch with the
totality of the Universe. As we
cherish life in every form, we manifest nothing but the joyful. Life is
forever, since life comes from God.
And when we learn to appreciate
the scope of life, we connect with
our own foreverness.

Affirmation

My life is filled with abundance.

November 28
Purity

One word that effectively describes the God aspect of us is *purity*. Our purity is the Divinity within, which is unsullied by negative thoughts, statements, or actions. The purity of us is able to look beyond fear to joy. Our purity is that area of us which enables our consciousness to achieve magnificence in our life experience.

Affirmation

I express my purity fully today.

November 29

Love

Love is the most complete abundance we can uncover within us. Love is of God, and when we express love we are expressing God. Today we can express love by being generous and kind to everyone we meet, having caring thoughts about every person and situation we encounter, nurturing our self.

Affirmation

I express the Love of God always.

November 30

Spiritual

> Our awareness of Spiritual Abundance awakens us and moves us along on our path to God. If we become overly connected to our physical world, through prayer and meditation we bring ourselves back to our Spiritual Source. Then as we live from our Source, we fully experience the abundance that life always reflects to us.

Affirmation

> I am a spiritually abundant child of God.

December

Spirituality

December 1
Individual

As we connect with our spiritual self, we begin to understand that it is our individual responsibility how quickly we move on our path. Although we are all connected to the One, each of us must discover God within ourselves. This individual process is an exciting, gratifying, fulfilling one that unites us with our brothers and sisters.

Affirmation

Today I discover the spirituality within me.

352

December 2

Others

We begin to share the spiritual nature of ourself by seeing it in others. Even if their actions belie the fact, everyone has God within. We don't have to help them see it; we only have to see it in them. This act alone helps our own spiritual nature grow, as well as that of everyone we encounter on our life's path.

Affirmation

I see the spiritual nature in everyone I meet.

December 3

Universe

We can reinforce our God connection by witnessing God at work in all living creatures and in inanimate objects as well. Spiritual growth entails our experiencing God everywhere present in our Universe. So when we are slopping through the rain on the way to a meeting we'd just as soon skip, that is the time to see God in everything.

Affirmation

I connect with God everywhere every day.

December 4

Compelling

The spiritual side of us tugs at us until we pay attention. We may be living a cavalier life in our material world, but there is always that compelling small voice within telling us that there is a better way to live. The wonderful part about that voice is that we don't have to do anything except listen to its wise, loving message.

Affirmation

Today I listen to the compelling Voice for God.

December 5

Integrating

It is seeing the world amiss to compartmentalize the various aspects of our life. When we begin our walk on our spiritual path, we see that work and play, a lover and a stranger, home and away all are governed by the same Universal Principles. When we integrate them into our life experience, we begin to live completely fulfilling lives.

Affirmation

I integrate all aspects of my life into oneness.

December 6

Discovery

What a discovery our spiritual nature is! We move from feeling we are living in an isolated little corner of the globe to feeling we are united with everyone we encounter, every experience we have. Spiritual discovery can be an activity with which we frequently connect. We rediscover God every millisecond with each new sensory input.

Affirmation

I open myself to more fully discovering God today.

December 7

Healing

We look for healing in doctors and medicines. All well and good, but that is focusing only on our bodies. True healing comes when we understand that our entirety—mind, body, spirit—is what we really work on. And it is only our spiritual connection that leads us to complete healing. God always sees everything as healed.

Affirmation

Today I experience healing energy in my entire being.

December 8

Attraction

When we open to it, we attract the spiritual in everything to us. When we block ourselves, we lure ego energy in our direction, and our lives seem not to work. As we connect with God, our lives are like magnets for all experiences to be joyful and uplifting. Our lives flow with ease and work wonderfully.

Affirmation

I attract only spiritual experiences to me.

December 9

Purpose

If we are seeking purpose in life, we haven't really connected with our spiritual self. Purpose comes from the vastness within, which is our God nature. When we are one with God, purpose doesn't have to be created. It merely is uncovered from within our beautiful inner self. Purpose then becomes our gentle guide.

Affirmation

I uncover my purpose today.

December 10

Flow

> There is a rhythm in our lives that comes from Universal Flow. When we release into it, our lives work with ease. But when we do it "our way," life becomes an ongoing struggle. The flow of life arises from the spiritual nature of everything, and all we need do is turn our free will in the direction of this Divine stream of consciousness.

Affirmation

> I am in the flow of life.

December 11
Love

Love is the essence of spirituality.
Love comes from God, and this unconditional love is the only way the
world will work perfectly. The exciting part of this is that we can begin
the process of healing our world by
extending love from ourselves. It is
important that we are aware of this
great power each moment of each
day.

Affirmation

My love heals the world.

December 12

Choice

Spirituality is a choice. It is one we make tens if not hundreds of times throughout each day. To choose spirituality is to choose God and to choose a life that works. When we opt for the spiritual life, we greatly uncomplicate our lives. As we become more spiritual, our planet moves closer to being healed.

Affirmation

Today I choose the spiritual life.

December 13
Shelter

If we are seeking shelter from the storm of life, we only need turn within to our spiritual essence. Our spirituality, our God-self, offers us all the protection we will ever need. Through our spirituality we can turn over all fears, all challenges we are facing. When we do, they are re-placed with solutions and a mar-velous serenity.

Affirmation

My spirituality gives me total shelter.

December 14
Abundance

The abundance of the Universe resides in spirituality. We can surround ourselves with things, but nothing makes us feel as rich as a deep God connection. As our spiritual nature matures, we realize there is abundance in every person, every object, every situation. And we feel this abundance every second of the day.

Affirmation

I am a spiritually abundant person.

December 15

Positive

A positive life is a spiritual life. It is
next to impossible to have a positive outlook on ourselves and the
world without a vibrant God connection. If we are awash in negativity, it is important to take time to
go within in prayer or meditation
and connect to God. With God all
things are possible . . . and positive.

Affirmation

I lead a positive, spiritual life.

December 16

Faith

We put our faith in many different areas of our life. We put our faith in relationships, in our job, in our home, in our hobby, in our bank account. But unless we put our faith in God, our lives will be essentially empty. Many of us worship the material world many years before we finally turn to the spirituality that is always within.

Affirmation

I place all my faith in God today.

December 17
Outreach

If we are worried about ourself all
the time, we don't have life in proper
perspective. When we come from
our spiritual nature, we reach out to
others as well as ourself. As we care
for others from our God-self, we
broaden our lives and announce to
the Universe that we are whole beings who are one with everyone.

Affirmation

I reach out to others today from my
God-self.

December 18

Energy

We are filled with energy when we are filled with spirituality. Energy is God stuff, and if we are lacking it we are falling short in our spirituality. A regimen of prayer and meditation, attending church, taking spiritual classes, inspirational reading will all serve to bring us back to a place where we are brimming over with God energy.

Affirmation

I nurture myself with God energy today.

December 19

Beauty

The next time we see someone new, let us truly look at the beauty beneath the surface. Have you ever noticed that someone's physical appearance ceases to matter once we get to know her. That's because we are knowing the real person, the spiritual being underneath. It is helpful if we look for that beauty from our first meeting.

Affirmation

Today I see the real beauty in others.

December 20

Innocence

The innocence of a child at play reflects the innate spirituality contained in that little being. Our busy world tends to cover up that innocence as we age, but it is still there within us. We close our eyes for a moment and imagine we are an innocent child at play again. Then we feel fully the spiritual magnificence behind that innocence.

Affirmation

I rediscover my innocence today.

December 21

Joy

The joy of life is the spirituality of life. When we are joyous, we are aware of the fullness of who we are spiritually. Our feeling comes from God, who created a joyful Universe in which we all can play. If we tire of playing, we are blocking our contact with our Creator. We simply have to turn once again to joy.

Affirmation

I always choose joy in my life.

December 22

Willing

If we wish to lead a spiritual life, we have to be willing. If we are unwilling to change the way we live any part of our life, then we are procrastinating in moving to a connection with our Universal Guide. Willingness comes when we admit to ourselves that our way just isn't working. We then know God's way does work.

Affirmation

I am willing to begin leading a spiritual life now.

December 23

Remembering

We generally don't remember who we are. When we do, we recall that we are sons and daughters of God. We remember that we came from perfection. We recollect that we are vessels replete with unconditional love. Remembering who we are is all we need do to lead a fully spiritual existence.

Affirmation

I remember who I am today.

December 24
Extending

> We arise in the morning fully in touch with our spirituality. If we start our day that way, we then move out into the day extending who we are and what we know to everyone we meet. Extending ourselves spiritually announces to ourselves and the world that we know who we are. We know we come from God.

Affirmation

> This day especially I extend my spirituality to others.

December 25

Light

> The Light of God surrounds us all.
> It is in us, through us, of us. The
> Light fills the new, the old, the all. It
> is the omniscience, omnipresence,
> omnipotence of God in all of exis-
> tence. We experienced the Light of
> God before we were born, we expe-
> rience it now, we will experience it
> when we lay down the body. It is
> ours to embrace.

Affirmation

> The Light of God fills me today.

December 26
Stillness

In the stillness is God. In the stillness we find our spirituality. If we
quiet our minds regularly each day,
we will discover God. As we take
time to be still, our creativity
emerges, life has meaning, we sail
through life. We need to release the
busy-ness of our ego that keeps our
mind whirling. In the stillness that
falls away.

Affirmation

I discover God in the stillness.

December 27
Teaching

Our spirituality emerges, not just for us but for everyone. When we begin to awaken spiritually, we are obligated to share our enlightening being with others. This is not a chore. It becomes a joy as we travel on our spiritual path. We become gentle teachers, not proselytizers. We share our God through unconditional love.

Affirmation

I share my spirituality with everyone.

December 28

Vision

Our vision is limited indeed when we are not aware of our spirituality. We limit ourselves to a narrow earth plane until we begin to awaken. Then we begin to extend our vision to all the Universe. When we connect with God, our vision for ourselves and others becomes magnificent. All we see is peace, joy, and love.

Affirmation

My spiritual vision is unlimited.

December 29

Knowing

There is eternal comfort in knowing that God is everywhere present, that we are perfect just the way we are. The more we open to God, the more we know the vast expanse of all there is to know. Our knowing gives us peace in all situations. Our knowing confirms our spiritual completeness.

Affirmation

My knowing always shows me God.

December 30

Awe

We stand in awe of the incredible depth and breadth of God. We cannot know Her expanse; we can know only that it is beyond any imaginings of ours. Our awe keeps us humble, gives us strength, extends our love. As we are in awe, we grow. As we are in awe, we expand. As we are in awe, we move toward self-completion.

Affirmation

I am in awe of God today and every day.

December 31

Ascent

Rather than imagining the close of a year as winding down, let us see it as ascent. We ascend beyond our limitations to an infinite view of our possibilities. We experience our spirituality in all its glory. We rise to meet the Love of God. We soar above the mundane sharing our God-self with all and everyone. We are complete.

Affirmation

I ascend to all the God possibilities that await me.

About the Author

DAVID STUART ALEXANDER is a writer of non-fiction and fiction. His background includes exploring the realm of his outer existence through fifteen years of traveling and living around the world, and exploring the realm of his inner existence and spiritual awakening through fifteen years of studying and experiencing metaphysical principles. He and his wife, bestselling author Joan Gattuso, teach, lecture, and present spiritual workshops, singly and together, across the USA and Canada, on the subjects of human potential, relationships, American Buddhism, *A Course in Miracles*, healing, and abundance.

For additional information about David Alexander and his presentations, telephone 1-800-256-8382.